CHINESE SHORT STORIES FOR BEGINNERS

20 Captivating Short Stories to Learn Chinese & Grow Your Vocabulary the Fun Way!

Easy Chinese Stories Vol. 2

Lingo Mastery

www.LingoMastery.com

TABLE OF CONTENTS

INTRODUCTION

Congratulations on your journey to learning Mandarin.

Like learning any other foreign language, it's going to open the doors for you to know more about Chinese culture. If you have been learning Mandarin for a while, you must have come across the concept of measure words which are used with nouns. One interesting fact is that the measure word for language in Chinese is "door." Isn't it amazing to know that even Chinese ancestors knew learning a new language would open another door for you?

Whether you are learning Mandarin for work, academic reasons or just for fun, the philosophy of the language will broaden your mind and give you a different view of life.

People around the world all say that Chinese is extremely difficult to learn. They are not wrong, but that's exactly what we're here for. This book has been written with your needs in mind, and it will help you on your journey to better your Mandarin.

What is this book about?

We've written this book to solve one big issue that seems to impact every new learner of the Chinese language—a lack of helpful and engaging reading material. There are tons (or gigabytes, in our modern terms) of easy and accessible learning materials when learning English, Spanish, French and German, etc., but unfortunately that's not the case with the Chinese language.

Our goal with this book will be to supply you with useful, entertaining, educational and challenging material that will not only allow you to learn the language but also help you pass the time and make the experience less formal and more fun—like any lesson should be. All the readings in the book are either stories from real life, or articles to you with educational facts about Western societies and Chinese society. We will not bore you with grammatical notes, spelling or structures: the readings have been well-written and revised to ensure that your attention will be caught.

Reading is a big aspect of improving your overall Chinese. Your vocabulary will broaden, and you will feel your Chinese improving whenever you pick up this book.

Stories for beginners? What does that mean?

We don't want the word to be misleading. When thinking about you as a beginner, we focused on combining two things:

1. Providing you with easy-to-understand words and structures;
2. Avoiding simplistic content.

To make things easier for you, we picked only common words—no rocket science, that's for sure. You won't encounter any complex sentences with multiple clauses and prepositions.

Just take the final step on your own—apply your diligence and work hard to get to the next level.

The suggested steps of working with this book

1. First, just read the story. Chances are you already know many words.
2. Then read it again, referring to the vocabulary. Note that our vocabulary is much easier to use than a conventional dictionary because:

a. the words are listed in the order of their appearance in the text;

b. the translations are given in the exact form you find them in the text;

c. the most complex words are given as word combinations to let you grasp the grammatical structure.

3. When you think you understand the major plot of the story, check by referring to the summary of the story that is provided both in Chinese and English.

4. Go over to the Questions section to check if you've understood the details.

5. Check if you were right in the Answers section.

6. And at last—time to enjoy. Read the story once again, getting pleasure from the feeling of great achievement. You deserve it!

What if I don't understand everything?

Remember—understanding each and every word is not your goal. Your goal is to grasp the essence of the story and enrich your vocabulary. It is **absolutely normal** that you may not understand some words or structures, and sometimes you may ultimately not entirely understand what the story is about.

Other recommendations for readers of Chinese Short Stories for Beginners Volume 2

Before we allow you to begin reading, we have a quick list of some other recommendations, tips and tricks for getting the best out of this book.

1. Read the stories without any pressure: feel free to return to the parts you didn't understand and take breaks when

necessary. This is like any fantasy, romance or sci-fi book you'd pick up, except with different goals.

2. Feel free to use any external material to make your experience more complete: while we've provided you with plenty of data to help you learn, you may feel obliged to look at textbooks or search for more helpful texts on the Internet—do not think twice about doing so! We even recommend it.

3. Find other people to learn with: while learning can be fun on your own, it definitely helps to have friends or family joining you on the tough journey of learning a new language. Find a like-minded person to accompany you in this experience, and you may soon find yourself competing to see which one of you can learn the most!

4. Try writing your own stories once you're done: all of the material in this book is made for you to learn not only how to read, but how to write as well. Like what you read? Try writing your own story now, and see what people think about it!

FREE BOOK!

Free Book Reveals The 6 Step Blueprint That Took Students

From Language Learners To Fluent In 3 Months

One last thing before we start. If you haven't already done it, head over to **LingoMastery.com/hacks** and grab a copy of our free book *Lingo Hacks*, which will teach you the important secrets you need to know to become fluent in a language as fast as possible. Again, you can find the free book at **LingoMastery.com/hacks**.

Now, without further ado, enjoy these 20 Chinese Stories for Beginners.

Good luck, reader!

CHAPTER 1

幼儿园的小朋友们 –
CHILDREN OF THE NURSERY

约翰逊是一个聪明可爱的英国小男孩。他今年七岁，是 2015 年 8 月在英国伦敦**出生**的。去年约翰逊六岁的时候，爸爸的公司**派**爸爸到上海的**分公司**工作，所以约翰逊和爸爸妈妈一起**搬**到了中国的上海。

每年夏天和**圣诞节**的时候，约翰逊会去英国看**爷爷奶奶**和**姥姥姥爷**。爷爷和奶奶住在**北方**的**约克郡**，姥姥和姥爷住在**布莱顿**的**海边**。

约翰逊现在上一所**国际幼儿园**的大班，今年九月份会成为一名**名副其实**的小学生。

约翰逊的班里一共有八个小朋友，他们**分别**是：约翰逊、乔治、大卫、尼古拉斯、伊莎贝拉、艾玛、苏菲亚和丽丽。**除了**丽丽**以外**，所有的小朋友都是在**外国**出生的。他们来中国的**原因**都是因为他们的爸爸妈妈现在在中国工作。丽丽的爸爸妈妈以前在美国**留学**和工作，在美国住了十年以后，他们**决定**回中国**发展**。丽丽是在中国出生的，可是爸爸妈妈**希望**丽丽可以**从小**讲一口**流利**的英文，所以他们送丽丽到这家国际幼儿园上学。

在幼儿园里，小朋友们和老师们都讲中文，每个星期他们也上五节英文课和五节**西班牙文**课。去年约翰逊刚来这家幼儿园的时候，一句中文也不会讲。几个月以后，**慢慢**地约翰逊可以听**懂**很多中文，也可以说一些。又过了几个月，约翰逊**几乎什么**都会说了。**好棒！**

说到西班牙文，尼古拉斯的爸爸妈妈是**西班牙**人，在家里尼古拉斯和他的爸爸妈妈用西班牙文**交流**。幼儿园儿里别的小朋友们就**不同**了，他们在一起玩儿的时候总是说中文。尼古拉斯**偶尔**也会**冒**一两句西班牙文出来，可是别的孩子们都会用中文**回复**，小朋友们只是在西班牙文课上练习说西班牙文。

幼儿园的小朋友们 – Children of the Nursery
With English Translation

约翰逊是一个聪明可爱的英国小男孩。他今年七岁，是 2015 年 8 月在英国伦敦出生的。

Yuēhànxùn shì yígè cōngmíng kě'ài de Yīngguó xiǎo nánhái. Tā jīnnián qī suì, shì 2015 nián 8 yuè zài Yīngguó Lúndūn **chūshēng** de.

Johnson is a smart and cute little English boy. He is seven years old and was **born** in London, England in August 2015.

去年约翰逊六岁的时候，爸爸的公司**派**爸爸到上海的**分公司**工作，所以约翰逊和爸爸妈妈一起**搬**到了中国的上海。

Qùnián Yuēhànxùn liù suì de shíhou, bàba de gōngsī **pài** bàba dào Shànghǎi de **fēn gōngsī** gōngzuò, suǒyǐ Yuēhànxùn hé bàba māma yìqǐ **bān** dàole Zhōngguó de Shànghǎi.

Last year, when Johnson was six years old, his father's company **sent** his father to work in the **branch** in Shanghai, so Johnson and his mother and father **moved** to Shanghai, China.

每年夏天和**圣诞节**的时候，约翰逊会去英国看**爷爷奶奶**和**姥姥姥爷**。爷爷和奶奶住在**北方**的**约克郡**，姥姥和姥爷住在**布莱顿**的**海边**。

Měinián xiàtiān hé **Shèngdànjié** de shíhou, Yuēhànxùn huì qù Yīngguó kàn **yéye nǎinai** hé **lǎolao lǎoyé**. Yéye hé nǎinai zhù zài **běifāng** de **Yuēkè Jùn**, lǎolao hé lǎoyé zhù zài **Bùláidùn** de **hǎibiān**.

Every summer and **Christmas**, Johnson would go to the UK to see his **paternal and maternal grandparents**. The paternal grandparents live in **Yorkshire** in the **North**, and the maternal grandparents live by the **sea** in **Brighton**.

约翰逊现在上一所**国际幼儿园**的大班，今年九月份会成为一名**名副其实**的小学生。

Yuēhànxùn xiànzài shàng yìsuǒ **guójì yòu'éryuán** de dàbān, jīnnián jiǔ yuèfèn huì chéngwéi yìmíng **míngfùqíshí** de xiǎoxuéshēng.

Johnson attends a class for older children at an **international nursery** and will be a real primary school student in September this year.

约翰逊的班里一共有八个小朋友，他们**分别**是：约翰逊、乔治、大卫、尼古拉斯、伊莎贝拉、艾玛、苏菲亚和丽丽。

Yuēhànxùn de bān lǐ yígòng yǒu bā gè xiǎopéngyǒu, tāmen **fēnbié** shì: Yuēhànxùn, Qiáozhì, Dà wèi, Nígǔlāsī, Yīshābèilā, Àimǎ, Sūfēiyà hé Lìli.

There are eight children in Johnson's class; they are, **respectively**: Johnson, George, David, Nicholas, Isabella, Emma, Sophia and Lili.

除了丽丽**以外**，所有的小朋友都是在**外国**出生的。他们来中国的**原因**都是因为他们的爸爸妈妈现在在中国工作。

Chúle Lìli **yǐwài**, suǒyǒu de xiǎopéngyǒu dōu shì zài **wàiguó** chūshēng de. Tāmen lái Zhōngguó de **yuányīn** dōu shì yīnwèi tāmen de bàba māma xiànzài zài Zhōngguó gōngzuò.

All the children were born **abroad except for** Lili. The **reason** they came to China is because their parents are both working in China now.

丽丽的爸爸妈妈以前在美国**留学**和工作，在美国住了十年以后，他们**决定**回中国**发展**。

Lìli de bàba māma yǐqián zài Měiguó **liúxué** hé gōngzuò, zài Měiguó zhùle shí nián yǐhòu, tāmen **juédìng** huí Zhōngguó **fāzhǎn**.

Lili's parents used to **study abroad** and work in the United States. After living in the United States for ten years, they **decided** to return to China to **develop** their careers.

丽丽是在中国出生的，可是爸爸妈妈**希望**丽丽可以从小讲一口**流利**的英文，所以他们送丽丽到这家国际幼儿园上学。

Lìli shì zài Zhōngguó chūshēng de, kěshì bàba māma **xīwàng** Lìli kěyǐ **cóngxiǎo** jiǎng yìkǒu **liúlì** de Yīngwén, suǒyǐ tāmen sòng Lìli dào zhè jiā guójì yòu'éryuán shàngxué.

Lili was born in China, but her parents **hoped** that she would speak **fluent** English **from a young age**, so they sent her to this international nursery.

在幼儿园里，小朋友们和老师们都讲中文，每个星期他们也上五节英文课和五节**西班牙文**课。

Zài yòu'éryuán lǐ, xiǎopéngyǒumen hé lǎoshīmen dōu jiǎng Zhōngwén, měi gè xīngqī tāmen yě shàng wǔ jié Yīngwén kè hé wǔ jié **Xībānyáwén** kè.

In the nursery, both the children and the teacher speak Chinese, and they also have five English lessons and five **Spanish** lessons every week.

去年约翰逊刚来这家幼儿园的时候，一句中文也不会讲。几个月以后，**慢慢地**约翰逊可以听**懂**很多中文，也可以说一些。

Qùnián Yuēhànxùn gāng lái zhè jiā yòu'éryuán de shíhou, yíjù Zhōngwén yě bú huì jiǎng. Jǐ gè yuè yǐhòu, **màn man de** Yuēhànxùn kěyǐ tīng **dǒng** hěnduō Zhōngwén, yě kěyǐ shuō yìxiē.

When Johnson first came to the nursery last year, he could not speak a word of Chinese. After a few months, Johnson **slowly began to understand** some Chinese, and could speak a little as well.

又过了几个月，约翰逊**几乎什么**都会说了。**好棒！**

Yòuguòle jǐ gè yuè, Yuēhànxùn **jīhū shénme** dōu huì shuō le.**Hǎo bàng**!

After a few more months, Johnson could say **almost everything. Great**!

说到西班牙文，尼古拉斯的爸爸妈妈是**西班牙**人，在家里尼古拉斯和他的爸爸妈妈用西班牙文**交流**。

Shuō dào Xībānyáwén, Nígǔlāsī de bàba māma shì **Xībānyá rén**, zài jiālǐ Nígǔlāsī hé tā de bàba māma yòng Xībānyáwén **jiāoliú**.

Speaking of Spanish, Nicholas' parents are **Spanish**, and Nicholas and his parents **communicate** in Spanish at home.

幼儿园里别的小朋友们就**不同**了，他们在一起玩儿的时候总是说中文。

Yòu'éryuán lǐ bié de xiǎopéngyǒumen jiù **bùtóng** le, tāmen zài yìqǐ wánr de shíhou zǒngshì shuō Zhōngwén.

The other children in the nursery are **different**; they always speak Chinese when they play together.

尼古拉斯**偶尔**也会**冒**一两句西班牙文出来，可是别的孩子们都会用中文**回复**，小朋友们只是在西班牙文课上练习说西班牙文。

Nígǔlāsī **ǒu'ěr** yě huì **mào** yì liǎng jù Xībānyáwén chūlái, kěshì bié de háizimen dōu huì yòng Zhōngwén **huífù**, xiǎopéngyǒumen zhǐshì zài Xībānyáwén kè shàng liànxí shuō Xībānyáwén.

Nicholas would **occasionally come up** with a sentence or two in Spanish, but the other children would **reply** in Chinese, and the children only practice speaking Spanish in Spanish lessons.

总结/Summary

约翰逊是一个七岁的英国小男孩。他和他的爸爸妈妈住在中国上海。他在一个国际幼儿园大班上学。在他的班里一共有八个小朋友，他们分别是：约翰逊、乔治、大卫、尼古拉斯、伊莎贝拉、艾玛、苏菲亚和丽丽。约翰逊刚来中国的时候一点儿中文也不会讲，慢慢地他可以听一些，然后可以说一些，又过了几个月，约翰逊中文说得很好了！小朋友们和老师们在幼儿园都讲中文，每个星期小朋友们也上五节英文课和五节西班牙文课。

Yuēhànxùn shì yígè qī suì de Yīngguó xiǎo nánhái. Tā hé tā de bàba māma zhù zài Zhōngguó Shànghǎi. Tā zài yígè guójì yòu'éryuán dàbān shàngxué. Zài tā de bān lǐ yígòng yǒu bā gè xiǎopéngyǒu, tāmen fēnbié shì: Yuēhànxùn, Qiáozhì, Dàwèi, Nígǔlāsī, Yīshābèilā, Àimǎ, Sūfēiyà hé Lìli. Yuēhànxùn gāng lái Zhōngguó de shíhou yìdiǎnr Zhōngwén yě bú huì jiǎng, màn man de tā kěyǐ tīng yìxiē, ránhòu kěyǐ shuō yìxiē, yòu guò le jǐ gè yuè, Yuēhànxùn Zhōngwén shuō dé hěn hǎo le! Xiǎopéngyǒumen hé lǎoshīmen zài yòu'éryuán dōu jiǎng Zhōngwén, měi gè xīngqī xiǎopéngyǒumen yě shàng wǔ jié Yīngwén kè hé wǔ jié Xībānyáwén kè.

Johnson is a seven-year-old English boy. He lives with his parents in Shanghai, China. He attends a class for older children in an international nursery. There are eight children in his class; they are: Johnson, George, David, Nicholas, Isabella, Emma, Sophia and Lili. When Johnson first came to China, he didn't speak any Chinese at all. Slowly he could understand some, and then he could speak some. After a few months, Johnson spoke Chinese very well! Both the children and the teachers speak Chinese in the nursery, and the children also have five English lessons and five Spanish lessons each week.

生词/Vocabulary List

- 出生 – **chūshēng**: to be born
- 派 – **pài**: to appoint, to send
- 分公司 – **fēn gōngsī**: branch, subsidiary
- 搬 – **bān**: to move
- 圣诞节 – **Shèngdànjié**: Christmas
- 爷爷 – **yéye**: paternal grandfather
- 奶奶 – **nǎinai**: paternal grandmother
- 姥爷 – **lǎoyé**: maternal grandfather
- 姥姥 – **lǎolao**: maternal grandmother
- 北方 – **běifāng**: North
- 约克郡 – **Yuēkèjùn**: Yorkshire
- 布莱顿 – **Bùláidùn**: Brighton
- 海边 – **hǎibiān**: seaside
- 国际 – **guójì**: international
- 幼儿园 – **yòu'éryuán**: nursery
- 名副其实 – **míngfùqíshí**: not in name only, but also in reality (idiom), real
- 分别 – **fēnbié**: respectively
- 除了…以外 – **chúle…yǐwài**: except, except for
- 外国 – **wàiguó**: foreign country, abroad
- 原因 – **yuányīn**: reason
- 留学 – **liúxué**: to study abroad
- 决定 – **juédìng**: to decide, to make up one's mind
- 发展 – **fāzhǎn**: to develop
- 希望 – **xīwàng**: to hope
- 从小 – **cóngxiǎo**: since childhood, from a young age
- 流利 – **liúlì**: fluent
- 西班牙文 – **Xībānyáwén**: Spanish
- 慢慢地 – **màn man de**: slowly
- 懂 – **dǒng**: to understand, to know
- 几乎 – **jīhū**: almost
- 什么 – **shénme**: whatever, everything
- 好棒 – **hǎo bàng**: Great! Awesome!
- 说到 – **shuō dào**: speaking of
- 西班牙 – **Xībānyá** : Spain

- 交流 – **jiāoliú**: to communicate
- 不同 – **bùtóng**: different
- 偶尔 – **ǒu'ěr**: occasionally
- 冒 – **mào**: to come up
- 回复 – **huífù**: to reply

问题/Questions

1. 为什么约翰逊住在中国上海?

   Why does Johnson live in Shanghai, China?

   A. 他和爸爸妈妈住在一起。
   B. 他是中国人。
   C. 他和爷爷奶奶住在一起。
   D. 他在中国上海上中学。

2. 约翰逊去一个中国幼儿园吗？

   Does Johnson go to a Chinese nursery?

   A. 对
   B. 错

3. 丽丽是在美国出生的。

   Lili was born in the United States.

   A. 对
   B. 错

4. 幼儿园的老师和小朋友们都说中文。

   The teachers and children in the nursery all speak Chinese.

   A. 对
   B. 错

5. 尼古拉斯会说一口流利的西班牙文。

   Nicholas can speak fluent Spanish.

   A. 对
   B. 错

答案/Answers

1. A 他和爸爸妈妈住在一起。
   He lives together with his mom and dad.

2. B 错
   False

3. B 错
   False

4. A 对
   True

5. A 对
   True

CHAPTER 2

幼儿园的饮食 – FOOD IN NURSERY

对于约翰逊**来说**，他最喜欢的是幼儿园的老师和小朋友们，然后他最喜欢的就是幼儿园的饭菜。

说起幼儿园的饭菜，我们要从英国的饭菜说起。来中国上海以前，从三岁开始约翰逊开始上**全天**的幼儿园。**大概**从那时起，约翰逊开始**记事**。

每天早上七点半爸爸送他去附近的幼儿园，到了幼儿园以后，第一件事是洗手，然后到幼儿园的**饭厅**吃早餐。早餐的选择有**麦片**加牛奶和**土司**。约翰逊的最爱是**巧克力口味**的麦片，很甜很好吃。约翰逊喜欢把麦片加到热牛奶里吃。约翰逊**对**土司**没有什么感觉**。在十点半的时候，老师会给小朋友们准备一两块**饼干**和一小杯果汁。果汁有苹果汁，橙汁和**菠萝汁**。

午饭的时间是中午十二点半。午饭经常是烤鸡块和**薯条**，**牛肉派**和薯条，**三明治**和**沙拉**，炸鱼和薯条，还有**意大利面**。当然了，还有一两个水果。饭厅里的水果盘里总是有**各种各样**的水果，如果小朋友们饿了或者想吃，**随时**都可以告诉老师。下午三点的时候，小朋友们吃**下午茶**。下午茶总是一个三明治。三明治有鸡蛋的，**奶酪**的和鸡肉的。约翰逊喜欢吃鸡蛋口味的。

下午五点，爸爸妈妈们会来幼儿园**接**小朋友们回家，晚饭在家里吃。

现在我们来说说上海幼儿园的饭菜。对于约翰逊来说，现在饭菜的**选择**多了很多。也许是因为现在的幼儿园很大，有两三百个小朋友，所以上海幼儿园的**厨房**和饭厅都很大，饭菜的**种类**也比伦敦幼儿园的多多了。

首先，在上海的幼儿园，**东西方饮食**的**比例**是一半一半。当然了，东方的饮食包括日本菜，**韩国菜**，**东南亚**菜和**印度**菜。这些国家的菜虽然和中餐有一些**相似**之处，可是它们的口味还是很不同的。我们就拿印度的**咖喱**和**泰国**的咖喱来说吧，印度的咖喱里面有各种各样的**香料**，它的味道有点**重**。泰国的咖喱就不同了，它里面有**椰奶**，跟印度的咖喱**比起来**，它的口味就**淡**了很多。**几乎**所有在约翰逊班里的小朋友们都喜欢吃泰国咖喱。

第二，在上海的幼儿园，早餐的选择实在是太多了！以前约翰逊早上只吃麦片加牛奶，现在在这里，约翰逊每个星期只有星期一和星期四吃两次麦片。星期二约翰逊吃**豆腐脑**和**油条**。星期三吃日本早餐，里面有白饭，一块烤**三文鱼**、一点**酱菜**，还有一份**味增汤**。星期五吃**广东早茶**。广东早茶吃很多各种各样的**点心**。约翰逊最喜欢吃的有**烧卖**，**虾饺**，**叉烧包**，**糯米鸡**和**皮蛋粥**等等。在上海的幼儿园，因为没有上午茶和下午茶，所以早饭和午饭的**分量**比伦敦的幼儿园会大一些。

最后，在上海的幼儿园，约翰逊吃到了很多很有**异国情调**的水果。在上海有很多从东南亚**进口**的水果，比如说**榴莲**，**山竹**，**蒲桃**，**火龙果**和**木瓜**等等。早餐和午餐在幼儿园总是有**水果拼盘**。

幼儿园的饮食 – Food in Nursery
With English Translation

对于约翰逊来说，他最喜欢的是幼儿园的老师和小朋友们，然后他最喜欢的就是幼儿园的饭菜。

Duìyú Yuēhànxùn **lái shuō**, tā zuì xǐhuān de shì yòu'éryuán de lǎoshī hé xiǎopéngyǒumen, ránhòu tā zuì xǐhuān de jiùshì yòu'éryuán de fàncài.

For Johnson, **he** likes the teachers and children in the nursery the most, and then after that his favorite thing in the nursery is the food.

说起幼儿园的饭菜，我们要从英国的饭菜说起。来中国上海以前，约翰逊从三岁开始上全天的幼儿园。大概从那时起，约翰逊开始记事。

Shuō qǐ yòu'éryuán de fàncài, wǒmen yào cóng Yīngguó de fàncài shuō qǐ. Lái Zhōngguó Shànghǎi yǐqián, Yuēhànxùn cóng sān suì kāishǐ shàng **quán tiān** de yòu'éryuán. **Dàgài** cóng nà shí qǐ, Yuēhànxùn kāishǐ **jìshì**.

Speaking of the nursery meals, we need to start with the British meals. Before coming to Shanghai, China, Johnson had started **full-time** nursery at the age of three. **Around** that time, Johnson started to **recall things**.

每天早上七点半爸爸送他去附近的幼儿园，到了幼儿园以后，第一件事是洗手，然后到幼儿园的饭厅吃早餐。

Měitiān zǎoshang qī diǎn bàn bàba sòng tā qù fùjìn de yòu'éryuán, dàole yòu'éryuán yǐhòu, dì yī jiàn shì shì xǐshǒu, ránhòu dào yòu'éryuán de **fàntīng** chī zǎocān.

At 7:30 every morning, his father took him to a nearby nursery. After arriving there, the first thing he did was to wash his hands, and then go to the **dining room** in the nursery for breakfast.

早餐的选择有**麦片**加牛奶和**土司**。约翰逊的最爱是**巧克力口味**的麦片，很**甜**很好吃。约翰逊喜欢把麦片加到热牛奶里吃。约翰逊对**土司没有什么感觉**。

Zǎocān de xuǎnzé yǒu **màipiàn** jiā niúnǎi hé **tǔsī**. Yuēhànxùn de zuì ài shì **qiǎokèlì kǒuwèi** de màipiàn, hěn **tián** hěn hào chī. Yuēhànxùn xǐhuān bǎ màipiàn jiā dào rè niúnǎi lǐ chī. Yuēhànxùn **duì** tǔsī **méiyǒu shénme gǎnjué**.

Breakfast options include **cereal** with milk and **toast**. Johnson's favorite is **chocolate-flavored** cereal, which is **sweet** and delicious. Johnson likes to eat cereal with hot milk. Johnson **doesn't like** toast.

在十点半的时候，老师会给小朋友们准备一两块**饼干**和一小杯果汁。果汁有苹果汁，橙汁和**菠萝汁**。

Zài shí diǎn bàn de shíhou, lǎoshī huì gěi xiǎopéngyǒumen zhǔnbèi yì liǎng kuài **bǐnggān** hé yì xiǎo bēi guǒzhī. Guǒzhī yǒu píngguǒ zhī, chéngzhī hé **bōluó** zhī.

At 10:30, the teachers prepare a **cookie** or two and a small glass of juice for the children. Juices are apple juice, orange juice or **pineapple** juice.

午饭的时间是中午十二点半。午饭经常是烤鸡块和**薯条**，牛肉派和薯条，三明治和**沙拉**，炸**鱼**和薯条, 还有**意大利面**。

Wǔfàn de shíjiān shì zhōngwǔ shí'èr diǎn bàn. Wǔfàn jīngcháng shì kǎojīkuài hé **shǔtiáo**, **niúròu pài** hé shǔtiáo, **sānmíngzhì** hé **shālā**, zháyú hé shǔtiáo, hái yǒu **yìdàlìmiàn**.

Lunch time is 12:30. For lunch, there are often grilled chicken nuggets and **french fries**, **beef pie** and fries, **sandwiches** and **salads**, fried fish and french fries, and **pasta**.

当然了，还有一两个水果。饭厅里的水果盘里总是有**各种各样**的水果，如果小朋友们饿了或者想吃，**随时**都可以告诉老师。

Dāngrán le, hái yǒu yì liǎng gè shuǐguǒ. Fàntīng lǐ de shuǐguǒ pán lǐ zǒngshì yǒu **gè zhǒng gè yàng** de shuǐguǒ, rúguǒ xiǎopéngyǒumen è le huòzhě xiǎng chī, **suíshí** dōu kěyǐ gàosù lǎoshī.

And of course, a fruit or two. There is always **a variety of** fruits in the fruit bowl in the dining room. If the children are hungry or want to eat, they can tell the teacher **at any time.**

下午三点的时候，小朋友们吃**下午茶**。下午茶总是一个三明治。三明治有鸡蛋的、**奶酪**的和鸡肉的。约翰逊喜欢吃鸡蛋口味的。

Xiàwǔ sān diǎn de shíhou, xiǎopéngyǒumen chī **xiàwǔ chá**. Xiàwǔ chá zǒngshì yígè sānmíngzhì. Sānmíngzhì yǒu jīdàn de, **nǎilào** de hé jīròu de. Yuēhànxùn xǐhuān chī jīdàn kǒuwèi de.

At three o'clock in the afternoon, the children have **afternoon tea**. Afternoon tea is always a sandwich. The sandwiches are egg, **cheese**, or chicken sandwiches. Johnson likes the egg ones.

下午五点，爸爸妈妈们会来幼儿园**接**小朋友们回家，晚饭在家里吃。

Xiàwǔ wǔ diǎn, bàba māmamen huì lái yòu'éryuán **jiē** xiǎopéngyǒumen huí jiā, wǎnfàn zài jiālǐ chī.

At five o'clock in the afternoon, parents will come to the nursery to **pick up** the children, then have dinner at home.

现在我们来说说上海幼儿园的饭菜。对于约翰逊来说，现在饭菜的**选择**多了很多。

Xiànzài wǒmen lái shuō shuō Shànghǎi yòu'éryuán de fàncài. Duìyú Yuēhànxùn lái shuō, xiànzài fàncài de **xuǎnzé** duōle hěnduō.

Now let's talk about the meals in the Shanghai nursery. For Johnson, there are now a lot more **choices** of meals.

也许是因为现在的幼儿园很大，有两三百个小朋友，所以上海幼儿园的**厨房**和饭厅都很大，饭菜的**种类**也比伦敦幼儿园的多多了。

Yěxǔ shì yīnwèi xiànzài de yòu'éryuán hěn dà, yǒu liǎng sānbǎi gè xiǎopéngyǒu, suǒyǐ Shànghǎi yòu'éryuán de **chúfáng** hé fàntīng dōu hěn dà, fàncài de **zhǒnglèi** yě bǐ Lúndūn yòu'éryuán de duō duōle.

Perhaps it is because his nursery is very large now, with two or three hundred children, so both the **kitchen** and dining room of the Shanghai nursery are very large. There is a much greater **variety** of meals than at the nursery in London.

首先，在上海的幼儿园，**东西方饮食**的**比例**是一半一半。当然了，东方的饮食包括日本菜，**韩国菜**，**东南亚菜**和**印度菜**。这些国家的菜虽然和中餐有一些**相似**之处，可是它们的口味还是很不同的。

Shǒuxiān, zài Shànghǎi de yòu'éryuán, **dōng xī fāng yǐnshí** de **bǐlì** shì yíbàn yíbàn. Dāngránle, Dōngfāng de yǐnshí bāokuò Rìběn cài, **Hánguó** cài, **Dōngnányà** cài hé **Yìndù** cài. Zhèxiē guójiā de cài suīrán hé zhōngcān yǒu yìxiē **xiāngsì** zhī chù, kěshì tāmen de kǒuwèi háishì hěn bùtóng de.

First of all, in the Shanghai nursery, **the ratio of Eastern and Western diets** is half and half. Of course, the Eastern diet includes Japanese, **Korean**, **Southeast Asian** and **Indian** food. Although the dishes of these countries have some **similarities** with Chinese food, their tastes are still very different.

我们就拿印度的**咖喱**和**泰国**的咖喱来说吧，印度的咖喱里面有各种各样的**香料**，它的味道有点**重**。泰国的咖喱就不同了，它里面有**椰奶**，跟印度的咖喱**比起来**，它的口味就**淡**了很多。**几乎**所有在约翰逊班里的小朋友们都喜欢吃泰国咖喱。

Wǒmen jiù ná Yìndù de **gālí** hé **Tàiguó** de gālí lái shuō ba, Yìndù de gālí lǐmiàn yǒu gè zhǒng gè yàng de **xiāngliào**, tā de wèidào yǒudiǎn **zhòng**. Tàiguó de gālí jiù bùtóng le, tā lǐmiàn yǒu **yē nǎi**, gēn Yìndù de gālí **bǐ qǐlái**, tā de kǒuwèi jiù **dàn**le hěnduō. Jīhū suǒyǒu zài Yuēhànxùn bān lǐ de xiǎopéngyǒumen dōu xǐhuān chī Tàiguó gālí.

Let's take Indian **curry** and **Thai** curry for example. Indian curry has all kinds of **spices** in it and its flavor is very strong. Thai curry is different, it has **coconut milk** in it, and it has a much **lighter** taste **compared to** Indian curry. **Almost** all the kids in Johnson's class love Thai curry.

第二，在上海的幼儿园，早餐的选择实在是太多了！以前约翰逊早上只吃麦片加牛奶，现在在这里，约翰逊每个星期只有星期一和星期四吃两次麦片。

Dì èr, zài Shànghǎi de yòu'éryuán, zǎocān de xuǎnzé shízài shì tài duō le! Yǐqián Yuēhànxùn zǎoshang zhǐ chī màipiàn jiā niúnǎi, xiànzài zài zhèlǐ, Yuēhànxùn měi gè xīngqī zhǐyǒu xīngqīyī hé xīngqīsì chī liǎng cì màipiàn.

Second, in the nursery in Shanghai, there are so many choices for breakfast! Johnson used to eat cereal and milk in the morning, but now in this nursery, Johnson only eats cereal twice a week, on Mondays and Thursdays.

星期二约翰逊吃**豆腐脑**和**油条**。星期三吃日本早餐，里面有白饭、一块烤三文鱼、一点**酱菜**，还有一份**味增汤**。

Xīngqī'èr Yuēhànxùn chī **dòufunǎo** hé **yóutiáo**. Xīngqīsān chī Rìběn zǎocān, lǐmiàn yǒu báifàn, yíkuài kǎo **sānwènyú**, yìdiǎn **jiàngcài**, hái yǒu yífèn **wèi zēng tāng**.

On Tuesdays, Johnson eats **bean curd** and **deep-fried dough sticks**. On Wednesdays, Johnson eats a Japanese breakfast, which has rice, a piece of grilled **salmon**, some **pickled vegetables**, and a portion of **miso soup**.

星期五吃**广东早茶**。广东早茶吃很多各种各样的**点心**。约翰逊最喜欢吃的有**烧卖**、**虾饺**、**叉烧包**、**糯米鸡**和**皮蛋粥**等等。

Xīngqīwǔ chī **Guǎngdōng zǎochá**. Guǎngdōng zǎochá chī hěnduō gè zhǒng gè yàng de **diǎnxīn**. Yuēhànxùn zuì xǐhuān chī de yǒu **shāomài**, **xiā jiǎo**, **chāshāo bāo**, **nuòmǐ jī** hé **pídàn zhōu děng děng**.

On Fridays, he eats **Cantonese morning tea**. Cantonese morning tea has many kinds of **dim sum**. Johnson's favorite dim sum are **siu mai**, **shrimp dumplings**, **barbecue pork buns**, **sticky rice chicken** and **fermented egg porridge, etc.**

在上海的幼儿园，因为没有上午茶和下午茶，所以早饭和午饭的**分量**比伦敦的幼儿园会大一些。

Zài Shànghǎi de yòu'éryuán, yīnwèi méiyǒu shàngwǔ chá hé xiàwǔ chá, suǒyǐ zǎofàn hé wǔfàn de **fènliàng** bǐ Lúndūn de yòu'éryuán huì dà yīxiē.

In Shanghai's nursery, because there is no morning tea and afternoon tea, the **portion** of breakfast and lunch is larger than that in the nursery in London.

最后，在上海的幼儿园，约翰逊吃到了很多很有**异国情调**的水果。在上海有很多从东南亚**进口**的水果，比如说**榴莲**、**山竹**、**蒲桃**、**火龙果**和**木瓜**等等。早餐和午餐在幼儿园总是有**水果拼盘**。

Zuìhòu, zài Shànghǎi de yòu'éryuán, Yuēhànxùn chī dào le hěnduō hěn yǒu **yìguó qíngdiào** de shuǐguǒ. Zài Shànghǎi yǒu hěnduō cóng Dōngnányà **jìnkǒu** de shuǐguǒ, bǐrú shuō **liúlián**, **shānzhú**, **pútáo**, **huǒlóngguǒ** hé **mùguā** děng děng. Zǎocān hé wǔcān zài yòu'éryuán zǒngshì yǒu **shuǐguǒ pīnpán**.

Finally, in the nursery in Shanghai, Johnson eats a lot of **exotic** fruits. There are many fruits **imported** from Southeast Asia in Shanghai, such as **durian, mangosteen, cattail, dragon fruit** and **papaya**, etc. There is always a **fruit platter** for breakfast and lunch in the nursery.

总结/Summary

对于约翰逊来说，伦敦幼儿园早餐的选择很少，总是麦片加牛奶和土司。午餐的选择有烤鸡块、炸鱼、牛肉派、三明治、意大利面和薯条等等。上海的幼儿园就不同了，选择多了很多，而且东西方饮食都有。早饭的选择有西方的麦片加牛奶和土司，也有东方的中式早饭，日本早餐和广东早茶。午餐的选择就更多了，有泰国菜、韩国菜和印度菜等等。在上海的幼儿园，约翰逊吃到了很多从东南亚进口的很有异国情调的水果。

Duìyú Yuēhànxùn lái shuō, Lúndūn yòu'éryuán zǎocān de xuǎnzé hěn shǎo, zǒngshì màipiàn jiā niúnǎi hé tǔsī. Wǔcān de xuǎnzé yǒu kǎo jī kuài, zhá yú, niúròu pài, sānmíngzhì, yìdàlìmiàn hé shǔ tiáo děng děng. Shànghǎi de yòu'éryuán jiù bùtóng le, xuǎnzé duō le hěnduō, érqiě dōngxīfāng yǐnshí dōu yǒu. Zǎofàn de xuǎnzé yǒu Xīfāng de màipiàn jiā niúnǎi hé tǔsī, yě yǒu Dōngfāng de zhōngshì zǎofàn, Rìběn zǎocān hé Guǎngdōng zǎochá. Wǔcān de xuǎnzé jiù gèng duō le, yǒu Tàiguó cài, Hánguó cài hé Yìndù cài děng děng. Zài Shànghǎi de yòu'éryuán, Yuēhànxùn chī dào le hěnduō cóng Dōngnányà jìnkǒu de hěn yǒu yìguó qíngdiào de shuǐguǒ.

For Johnson, London nursery's breakfast options are few; it is always cereal with milk and toast. Lunch options include grilled chicken nuggets, fried fish, beef pies, sandwiches, pasta and chips, etc. The nursery in Shanghai is different, there are many choices, and there are both Eastern and Western foods. Breakfast options include Western cereal with milk and toast, as well as Eastern Chinese breakfast, Japanese breakfast, and Cantonese morning tea. There are more choices for lunch, with Thai, Korean and Indian dishes to name a few. At the nursery in Shanghai, Johnson eats a lot of exotic fruits imported from Southeast Asia.

生词/Vocabulary List

- 对于…来说 – duìyú…lái shuō: for
- 全天 – quán tiān: full-day
- 大概 – dàgài: perhaps
- 记事 – jìshì: to remember things
- 饭厅 – fàntīng: dining room
- 麦片 – màipiàn: cereal
- 土司 – tǔsī: toast
- 巧克力 – qiǎokèlì: chocolate
- 口味 – kǒuwèi: taste, flavor
- 甜 – tián: sweet
- 没有什么感觉 – méiyǒu shénme gǎnjué: do not have strong feelings for something
- 饼干 – bǐnggān: biscuit
- 菠萝汁 – bōluó zhī: pineapple juice
- 薯条 – shǔ tiáo: fries
- 牛肉派 – niúròu pài: beef pie
- 三明治 – sānmíngzhì: sandwich
- 沙拉 – shālā: salad
- 意大利面 – yìdàlìmiàn: pasta
- 各种各样 – gè zhǒng gè yàng: all kinds of, all types of
- 下午茶 – xiàwǔ chá: afternoon tea
- 奶酪 – nǎilào: cheese
- 接 – jiē: to pick up
- 选择 – xuǎnzé: choice
- 厨房 – chúfáng: kitchen
- 种类 – zhǒnglèi: type
- 东西方 – dōng xī fāng: East-West
- 饮食 – yǐnshí: diet
- 比例 – bǐlì: proportion
- 韩国 – Hánguó: Korea
- 东南亚 – Dōngnányà: Southeast Asia
- 印度 – Yìndù: India
- 相似 – xiāngsì: similarity
- 咖喱 – gālí: curry
- 泰国 – Tàiguó: Thailand
- 香料 – xiāngliào: spices
- 重 – zhòng: strong
- 椰奶 – yē nǎi: coconut milk
- 比起来 – bǐ qǐlái: to be compared with
- 几乎 – jīhū: almost

- 豆腐脑 – dòufu nǎo: bean curd
- 油条 – yóutiáo: deep-fried dough sticks
- 三文鱼 – sānwènyú: salmon
- 酱菜 – jiàngcài: pickled vegetables
- 味增汤 – wèi zēng tang: miso soup
- 广东早茶 – Guǎngdōng zǎochá: Cantonese morning tea
- 点心 – diǎnxīn: dim sum
- 烧卖 – shāomài: sio mai
- 虾饺 – xiā jiǎo: shrimp dumplings
- 叉烧包 – chāshāo bāo: barbeque pork buns
- 糯米鸡 – nuòmǐ jī: sticky rice chicken
- 皮蛋粥 – pídàn zhōu: fermented egg porridge
- 等等 – děng děng：etc.
- 分量 – fènliàng: portion
- 异国情调 – yìguó qíngdiào: exotic
- 榴莲 – liúlián: durian
- 山竹 – shānzhú: mangosteen
- 蒲桃 – pútáo: cattail
- 火龙果 – huǒlóng guǒ: dragon fruit
- 木瓜 – mùguā: papaya
- 水果拼盘 – shuǐguǒ pīnpán: fruit platter

问题/Questions

1. 约翰逊喜欢加麦片到热牛奶里吃。

   Johnson likes to add cereal to hot milk to eat it.

   A. 对
   B. 错

2. 在伦敦幼儿园，小朋友们在幼儿园吃晚餐。

   In the London nursery, children eat dinner there.

   A. 对
   B. 错

3. 约翰逊最喜欢的三明治是奶酪口味的。

   Johnson's favorite sandwich is cheese.

   A. 对
   B. 错

4. 在上海的幼儿园，小朋友们星期五早餐吃什么？

   In the nursery in Shanghai, what do children eat for breakfast on Fridays?

   A. 日本早餐
   B. 豆腐脑和油条
   C. 广东早茶
   D. 麦片和牛奶

5. 约翰逊在上海幼儿园吃过很多从东南亚进口的水果。

   Johnson ate a lot of fruits imported from Southeast Asia in the Shanghai nursery.

   A. 对
   B. 错

答案/Answers

1. A 对
   True

2. B 错
   False

3. B 错
   False

4. C 广东早茶
   Cantonese morning tea

5. C 对
   True

CHAPTER 3

艾玛的生日派对 –
EMMA'S BIRTHDAY PARTY

艾玛下个月十号就七岁了！艾玛很**期盼**她的生日**派对**！

爸爸妈妈从两个月前就开始**准备**这个生日派对了，所以艾玛知道派对一定会很大也会很**成功**。早早地艾玛就知道她想**邀请**七十个小朋友来她的生日派对。为什么是七十个呢？因为是她七岁的生日。哈哈！哈哈！妈妈还说准备这个**名单**是艾玛**唯一**的**任务**。

再简单不过了！

在幼儿园里艾玛一共认识十五个小朋友，七个是艾玛班里的，还有八个是**隔壁**班的。每个周末艾玛和爸爸妈妈去**教堂**，在教堂里艾玛还认识大概二十个小朋友。他们的**年龄**都和艾玛**相仿**，能和艾玛玩到一块儿。在爸爸妈妈**公司**里艾玛也认识几个小朋友，大概十个。艾玛还想邀请住在**同一个小区**里的一些小朋友，最后的几个是艾玛在**芭蕾舞俱乐部**的小朋友。加起来，**刚刚好好**七十个小朋友。**任务完成**了！

生日派对的**地点**是在小区的**活动中心**。爸爸妈妈很早就把活动中心**预订**了。爸爸妈妈的任务太多了！除了预定活动中心以外，还要**发邀** 请函，**装饰**活动中心，预订生日派对的晚餐和**饮料**，最重要的是还要**计划**派对当晚的**娱乐活动**。艾玛的爸爸**提出**了一个很好的**建议**：可以找一个**专门负责筹备**派对的**策划师**来筹备艾玛的生日派对。妈妈一听到这个建议就**举**双手**赞成**。派对的策划师很快就找到了，爸爸妈妈的任务完成了。

现在离下个月十号还有五个星期，策划师说准备时间很**充足**。

策划师很有**经验**，而且她也有很多**生意伙伴**。生意伙伴中有**开娱**乐公司的，有在**餐饮行业**的，还有开**室内**装饰公司的。策划师提出了三个不同的**服务组合**，这三个组合有不同的**价位**。越贵的价位**包括**越多的**服务项目**。艾玛的爸爸妈妈选了最贵的那个，因为他们想让艾玛有一个最**难忘**的七岁生日派对。

艾玛的生日派对 – Emma's Birthday Party
With English Translation

艾玛下个月十号就七岁了！艾玛很**期盼**她的生日**派对**！

Àimǎ xià gè yuè shí hào jiù qī suì le! Àimǎ hěn **qīpàn** tā de shēngrì **pàiduì**!

Emma will be seven years old on the tenth of next month! Emma is **looking forward to** her birthday **party**!

爸爸妈妈从两个月前就开始**准备**这个生日派对了，所以艾玛知道派对一定会很大也会很**成功**。早早地艾玛就知道她想**邀请**七十个小朋友来她的生日派对。

Bàba māma cóng liǎng gè yuè qián jiù kāishǐ **zhǔnbèi** zhège shēngrì pàiduì le, suǒyǐ Àimǎ zhīdào pàiduì yídìng huì hěn dà yě huì hěn **chénggōng**. Zǎo zǎo de Àimǎ jiù zhīdào tā xiǎng **yāoqǐng** qīshí gè xiǎopéngyǒu lái tā de shēngrì pàiduì.

Mom and Dad have been **preparing** this birthday party since two months ago, so Emma knew it was going to be big and **successful**. Emma knew early on that she wanted to **invite** seventy children to her birthday party.

为什么是七十个呢？因为是她七岁的生日。哈哈！哈哈！妈妈还说准备这个**名单**是艾玛**唯一**的**任务**。

Wèishénme shì qīshí gè ne? Yīnwèi shì tā qī suì de shēngrì. Hāhā! Hāhā! Māma hái shuō zhǔnbèi zhège **míngdān** shì Àimǎ **wéiyī** de **rènwù**.

Why seventy? Because it is her seventh birthday. Ha ha ha ha! Mom also said that preparing the **list** was Emma's **only task**.

再简单不过了！

Zài jiǎndān búguòle!
It couldn't be easier!

在幼儿园里艾玛一共认识十五个小朋友，七个是艾玛班里的，还有八个是**隔壁**班的。每个周末艾玛和爸爸妈妈去**教堂**，在教堂里艾玛还认识大概二十个小朋友。他们的**年龄**都和艾玛**相仿**，能和艾玛玩到一块儿。

Zài yòu'éryuán lǐ Àimǎ yígòng rènshí shíwǔ gè xiǎopéngyǒu, qī gè shì Àimǎ bān lǐ de, hái yǒu bā gè shì **gébì** bān de. Měi gè zhōumò Àimǎ hé bàba māma qù **jiàotáng**, zài jiàotáng lǐ Àimǎ hái rènshí dàgài èrshí gè xiǎopéngyǒu. Tāmen de **niánlíng** dōu hé Àimǎ **xiāngfǎng**, néng hé Àimǎ wán dào yíkuàir.

In the nursery, Emma knows a total of fifteen children, seven from her class and eight from the **next-door** class. Every weekend Emma and her parents go to **church**, where she also knows about twenty children. They are all about **the same age** as her and could play well together.

在爸爸妈妈**公司**里艾玛也认识几个小朋友，大概十个。艾玛还想邀请住在**同一个小区**里的一些小朋友，最后的几个是艾玛在**芭蕾舞俱乐部**的小朋友。加起来，**刚刚好好**七十个小朋友。任务**完成**了！

Zài bàba māma **gōngsī** lǐ Àimǎ yě rènshí jǐ gè xiǎopéngyǒu, dàgài shí gè. Àimǎ hái xiǎng yāoqǐng zhù zài **tóng yígè xiǎoqū** lǐ de yìxiē xiǎopéngyǒu, zuìhòu de jǐ gè shì Àimǎ zài **bālěiwǔ jùlèbù** de xiǎopéngyǒu. Jiā qǐlái, **gānggāng hǎohǎo** qīshí gè xiǎopéngyǒu. Rènwù **wánchéng**le!

Emma also knows a few children in Mom and Dad's **company**, about ten or so. Emma also wants to invite some children who live in **the same community**, and the last few are the children from Emma's

ballet club. In total, there are **exactly** seventy children. Mission **accomplished**!

生日派对的**地点**是在小区的**活动中心**。爸爸妈妈很早就把活动中心**预订**了。爸爸妈妈的任务太多了！

Shēngrì pàiduì de dìdiǎn shì zài xiǎoqū de **huódòng zhōngxīn**. Bàba māma hěn zǎo jiù bǎ huódòng zhōngxīn **yùdìng**le. Bàba māma de rènwù tài duō le!

The **venue** for the birthday party will be the **activity center** of the community. Mom and Dad **booked** the activity center very early. Mom and Dad have too many tasks!

除了预定活动中心以外，还要**发邀请函**，装饰活动中心，预订生日派对的晚餐和**饮料**，最重要的是还要**计划**派对当晚的**娱乐活动**。

Chúle yùdìng huódòng zhōngxīn yǐwài, hái yào **fā yāoqǐng hán**, **zhuāngshì** huódòng zhōngxīn, yùdìng shēngrì pàiduì de wǎncān hé **yǐnliào**, zuì zhòngyào de shì hái yào **jìhuà** pàiduì dāngwǎn de **yúlè huódòng**.

In addition to booking the event center, they also need to **send out invitations**, **decorate** the event center, book dinner and **drinks** for the birthday party, and most importantly, **plan** the **entertainment** for the night.

艾玛的爸爸**提出**了一个很好的**建议**：可以找一个**专门负责筹备**派对的**策划师**来筹备艾玛的生日派对。妈妈一听到这个建议就**举双手赞成**。

Àimǎ de bàba **tíchū**le yígè hěn hǎo de **jiànyì**: Kěyǐ zhǎo yígè **zhuānmén fùzé chóubèi** pàiduì de **cèhuà shī** lái chóubèi Àimǎ de shēngrì pàiduì. Māma yì tīng dào zhège jiànyì jiù **jǔ** shuāngshǒu **zànchéng**.

Emma's dad **proposed** a good suggestion: Find a **specialized party planner** to **plan** Emma's birthday party. Mom **raised** both of her hands **in approval** as soon as she heard the suggestion.

派对的策划师很快就找到了，爸爸妈妈的任务完成了。

Pàiduì de cèhuà shī hěn kuài jiù zhǎodàole, bàba māma de rènwù wánchéngle.

The planner for the party was quickly found, and Mom and Dad's task was accomplished.

现在离下个月十号还有五个星期，策划师说准备时间很**充足**。

Xiànzài lí xià gè yuè shí hào hái yǒu wǔ gè xīngqī, cèhuà shī shuō zhǔnbèi shíjiān hěn **chōngzú**.

There are still five weeks before the tenth of next month, and the planner said that there is **plenty** of time to prepare.

策划师很有**经验**，而且她也有很多**生意伙伴**。生意伙伴中有开娱乐公司的，有在**餐饮行业**的，还有开**室内**装饰公司的。

Cèhuà shī hěn yǒu **jīngyàn**, érqiě tā yě yǒu hěnduō **shēngyì huǒbàn**. Shēngyì huǒbàn zhōng yǒu **kāi** yúlè gōngsī de, yǒu zài **cānyǐn hángyè** de, hái yǒu kāi **shìnèi** zhuāngshì gōngsī de.

The planner is very **experienced**, and she also has many **business partners**. Among the business partners, there are people who **run** entertainment companies, **catering companies** and **interior** design companies.

策划师提出了三个不同的**服务组合**，这三个组合有不同的**价位**。越贵的价位**包括**越多的**服务**项目。艾玛的爸爸妈妈选了最贵的那个，因为他们想让艾玛有一个最**难忘**的七岁生日派对。

Cèhuà shī tíchūle sān gè bùtóng de **fúwù zǔhé**, zhè sān gè zǔhé yǒu bùtóng de **jiàwèi**. Yuè guì de jiàwèi **bāokuò** yuè duō de **fúwù**

xiàngmù. Àimǎ de bàba māma xuǎnle zuì guì de nàgè, yīnwèi tāmen xiǎng ràng Àimǎ yǒu yígè zuì **nánwàng** de qī suì shēngrì pàiduì.

The planners came up with three different **service packages**, all at different **price levels**. The more expensive the price, the more **service items** are **included**. Emma's parents chose the most expensive one because they wanted Emma to have the most **memorable** seventh birthday party.

总结/Summary

艾玛下个月十号就七岁了！爸爸妈妈想给艾玛开一个又大又成功的生日派对。艾玛准备邀请七十个小朋友来参加她的生日派对。为了准备生日派对，爸爸妈妈有太多的事情要准备了。他们要预订小区的活动中心，发邀请函，预订派对的晚餐和饮料，还要计划派对当晚的娱乐活动。最后爸爸建议找一个专门负责筹划生日派对的策划师，妈妈听到后举双手赞成。策划师说五个星期的准备时间很充足。策划书提出了三个不同价位的服务组合，爸爸妈妈选了最贵的一个，因为他们想让艾玛有一个难忘的七岁生日派对。

Àimǎ xià gè yuè shí hào jiù qī suì le! Bàba māma xiǎng gěi Àimǎ kāi yígè yòu dà yòu chénggōng de shēngrì pàiduì. Àimǎ zhǔnbèi yāoqǐng qīshí gè xiǎopéngyǒu lái cānjiā tā de shēngrì pàiduì. Wèile zhǔnbèi shēngrì pàiduì, bàba māma yǒu tài duō de shìqíng yào zhǔnbèile. Tāmen yào yùdìng xiǎoqū de huódòng zhōngxīn, fā yāoqǐng hán, yùdìng pàiduì de wǎncān hé yǐnliào, hái yào jìhuà pàiduì dāngwǎn de yúlè huódòng. Zuìhòu bàba jiànyì zhǎo yígè zhuānmén fùzé chóuhuà shēngrì pàiduì de cèhuà shī, māma tīng dào hòu jǔ shuāngshǒu zànchéng . Cèhuà shī shuō wǔ gè xīngqī de zhǔnbèi shíjiān hěn chōngzú. Cèhuà shū tíchūle sān gè bùtóng jiàwèi de fúwù zǔhé, bàba māma xuǎnle zuì guì de yígè, yīnwèi tāmen xiǎng ràng Àimǎ yǒu yígè nánwàng de qī suì shēngrì pàiduì.

Emma will be seven years old on the tenth of next month! Mom and Dad want to throw Emma a big and successful birthday party. Emma is going to invite seventy children to her birthday party. Mom and Dad have so many things to prepare for the birthday party. They need to book the community's event center, send out invitations, book dinner and drinks for the party, and plan the entertainment for the night of the party. In the end, Emma's Dad suggested finding a planner who specializes in birthday parties, and Emma's Mom raised her hands in approval after hearing it. The party planner says five weeks is plenty of time to prepare. The planner proposed three service packages at different price points, and Mom and Dad chose the most expensive one because they wanted Emma to have an unforgettable seventh birthday party.

生词/Vocabulary List

- 期盼 – qīpàn: to look forward to
- 派对 – pàiduì: party
- 准备 – zhǔnbèi: to prepare, preparation
- 成功 – chénggōng: to succeed, success
- 邀请 – yāoqǐng: to invite
- 名单 – míngdān: list
- 唯一 – wéiyī: only
- 任务 – rènwù: task
- 再简单不过了 – zài jiǎndān búguò le: couldn't be simpler
- 隔壁 – gébì: next door
- 教堂 – jiàotáng: church
- 年龄 – niánlíng: age
- 相仿 – xiāngfǎng: similar
- 公司 - gōngsī: company
- 同一个 – tóng yígè: the same
- 小区 – xiǎoqū: community
- 芭蕾舞 – bālěiwǔ: ballet
- 俱乐部 – jùlèbù: club
- 刚刚好好 – gānggāng hǎohǎo: exactly
- 完成 – wánchéng: to finish, to complete, to accomplish
- 地点 – dìdiǎn: place, venue
- 活动 – huódòng: activity
- 中心 – zhōngxīn: center
- 预订 – yùdìng: to book
- 发 – fā: to send out
- 邀请函 – yāoqǐng hán: invitation card
- 装饰 – zhuāngshì: to decorate, decoration
- 饮料 – yǐnliào: drinks
- 计划 – jìhuà: to plan, plan
- 娱乐 – yúlè: entertainment
- 提出 – tíchū: to propose
- 建议 – jiànyì: to suggest, to recommend
- 专门 – zhuānmén: specially
- 负责 – fùzé: to be responsible for
- 筹备 – chóubèi: to arrange, to prepare
- 策划师 – cèhuà shī: planner
- 举 – jǔ: to raise
- 赞成 – zànchéng: to approve
- 经验 – jīngyàn: to experience, experience

- 生意 – shēngyì: business
- 伙伴 – huǒbàn: partner
- 开 – kāi: to open, to run
- 餐饮 – cānyǐn: food and drink
- 行业 – hángyè: industry, profession
- 室内 – shìnèi: indoor
- 服务 – fúwù: to serve, service
- 组合 – zǔhé: package, combination
- 价位 – jiàwèi: price level
- 包括 – bāokuò: to include
- 服务项目 – fúwù xiàngmù: service items
- 难忘 – nánwàng: memorable

问题/Questions

1. 下个月十五号艾玛就七岁了！

   Emma will be seven years old on the fifteenth of next month!

   A. 对
   B. 错

2. 艾玛唯一的任务是做什么？

   What is Emma's only task?

   A. 准备邀请函的名单。
   B. 发邀请函。
   C. 预订派对的晚餐和饮料。
   D. 计划派对当晚的娱乐活动。

3. 艾玛一共邀请了多少小朋友来参加她的生日派对。

   How many children has Emma invited to her birthday party?

   A. 四十个小朋友
   B. 五十个小朋友
   C. 六十个小朋友
   D. 七十个小朋友

4. 派对的策划师一共有几个星期准备艾玛的生日派对？

   How many weeks does the party planner have to prepare
   Emma's birthday party?

   A. 一个星期
   B. 三个星期
   C. 四个星期
   D. 五个星期

5. 艾玛的爸爸妈妈选了最贵的服务组合。

   Emma's parents chose the most expensive service package.

   A. 对
   B. 错

答案/Answers

1. B 错
   False

2. A 准备邀请函的名单。
   To prepare the invitation list.

3. D 七十个小朋友
   Seventy children

4. D 五个星期
   Five weeks

5. A 对
   True

CHAPTER 4

西湖一日游 – WEST LAKE DAY TOUR

约翰逊的小学每年都会**组织春游**。**立春**以后，**植物**开始**发芽生长**，许多**鲜花开放**。春季是**万物复苏**的季节。

今年约翰逊小学的春游**定**在三月十八号，是**杭州西湖一日游**。学生们早就**等不及了**！

春游当天，学生们还像**往常**一样去了小学，然后小学的**校车**把学生和老师们送到了上海**高铁站**。从上海到杭州坐高铁只要一个小时。高铁站好大呀！里面的人太多了！学生们**排好队**，有**秩序**地跟在老师后面走。老师和学生们背上都**背着旅行包**，旅行包里**装满**了好吃的，好喝的和一些一日游**必备品**。

高铁很**新**，**座位**很**软**很舒服。高铁的**时速**是在二百五十**公里**到三百五十公里之间，**车厢**是**超静音**的。上午刚过十点，学生和老师们就已经**到达**了杭州高铁站。在高铁站**出口**，老师和学生们**直接**坐上学校早早**安排**好的一辆旅游**大客车**，**目的地**是杭州西湖。

学校**考虑**到学生们年纪小，**体力有限**，所以把春游的主要活动定为坐**游览船**。游览船从西湖的东边开船，**顺时针方向**游**遍**西湖的南边、西边和北边，最后回到**最初**的开船处。对于老年人和小孩来说，在西湖坐游览船是很**流行**的。在**欣赏**西湖的美景的同时，他们还可以吃午餐和聊天儿。西湖很大，等游览船回到东边时，已经是下午三点半了。四个小时**不知不觉**地就过去了！

学生们晚上到家时已经七点了！多么好玩儿的春游啊！

西湖一日游– West Lake Day Tour
With English Translation

约翰逊的小学每年都会**组织春游**。立春以后，**植物**开始**发芽生长**，许多**鲜花开放**。春季是**万物复苏**的季节。

Yuēhànxùn de xiǎoxué měi nián dōu huì zǔzhī **chūnyóu**. **Lìchūn** yǐhòu, **zhíwù** kāishǐ **fāyá shēngzhǎng**, xǔduō **xiānhuā kāifàng**. Chūnjì shì **wànwù fùsū** de jìjié.

Johnson's primary school **organizes** a **spring outing** every year. After the **beginning of spring**, **plants** begin to **sprout** and **grow**, and many **fresh flowers bloom**. Spring is the season of **revival of all things**.

今年约翰逊小学的春游**定**在三月十八号，是**杭州西湖一日游**。学生们早就**等不及了**！

Jīnnián Yuēhànxùn xiǎoxué de chūnyóu **dìng** zài sān yuè shíbā hào, shì **Hángzhōu Xīhú yí rì yóu**. Xuéshēngmen zǎo jiù **děng bùjíle**!

This year's spring outing at Johnson's primary school is **scheduled** for March 18, a **one-day trip to the West Lake in Hangzhou**. Students **can't wait**!

春游当天，学生们还像**往常**一样去了小学，然后小学的**校车**把学生和老师们送到了上海**高铁站**。从上海到杭州坐高铁只要一个小时。高铁站好大呀！里面的人太多了！

Chūnyóu dāngtiān, xuéshēngmen hái xiàng **wǎngcháng** yíyàng qùle xiǎoxué, ránhòu xiǎoxué de **xiàochē** bǎ xuéshēng hé lǎoshīmen sòng dàole Shànghǎi **gāotiě zhàn**. Cóng Shànghǎi dào Hángzhōu zuò gāotiě zhǐyào yígè xiǎoshí. Gāotiě zhàn hǎo dà ya! Lǐmiàn de rén tài duō le!

On the day of the spring tour, the students went to the primary school **as usual**, and then the **school bus** took the students and teachers to the Shanghai **high-speed rail station**. It only takes one hour by high-speed train from Shanghai to Hangzhou. The high-speed rail station is so big! There are so many people inside!

学生们**排好队**，有**秩序**地跟在老师后面走。老师和学生们**背上**都**背着旅行包**，旅行包里**装满**了好吃的，好喝的和一些一日游**必备品**。

Xuéshēngmen **pái hǎo duì**, yǒu **zhìxù** de gēn zài lǎoshī hòumiàn zǒu. Lǎoshī hé xuéshēngmen **bèi shàng** dōu **bēi**zhe **lǚxíng bāo**, lǚxíng bāo lǐ **zhuāng mǎn**le hǎo chī de, hǎo hē de hé yìxiē yí rì yóu **bìbèi pǐn**.

The students **lined up** and followed the teacher in an **orderly manner**. Every teacher and student **carried travel bags on their back**, **full of** food, drinks and some day trip **essentials**.

高铁很**新**，**座位**很**软**很舒服。高铁的**时速**是在二百五十公里到三百五十公里之间，**车厢**是**超静音**的。

Gāotiě hěn **xīn**, **zuòwèi** hěn **ruǎn** hěn shūfu. Gāotiě de **shísù** shì zài èrbǎi wǔshí gōnglǐ dào sānbǎi wǔshí gōng lǐ zhī jiān, **chēxiāng** shì **chāo jìngyīn** de.

The high-speed rail is very **new**, and the **seats** are **soft** and comfortable. The **speed** of the high-speed rail is between 250 and 350 kilometers per hour, and the **carriages** are **ultra-quiet**.

上午刚过十点，学生和老师们就已经**到达**了杭州高铁站。在高铁站**出口**，老师和学生们**直接**坐上学校早早**安排**好的一辆旅游**大客车**，**目的地**是杭州西湖。

Shàngwǔ gāng guò shí diǎn, xuéshēng hé lǎoshīmen jiù yǐjīng **dàodá**le Hángzhōu gāotiě zhàn. Zài gāotiě zhàn **chūkǒu**, lǎoshī hé xuéshēngmen **zhíjiē** zuò shàng xuéxiào zǎozǎo **ānpái** hǎo de yíliàng lǚyóu **dà kèchē**, **mùdìdì** shì Hángzhōu Xīhú.

Just after ten o'clock in the morning, the students and teachers **arrived** at the Hangzhou high-speed railway station. At the **exit** of the high-speed railway station, teachers and students **immediately** boarded a **coach arranged** by the school in advance, and the **destination** was West Lake in Hangzhou.

学校**考虑**到学生们年纪小，**体力有限**，所以把春游的主要活动定为坐**游览船**。游览船从西湖的东边开船，**顺时针方向游遍**西湖的南边，西边和北边，最后回到**最初**的开船处。

Xuéxiào **kǎolǜ** dào xuéshēngmen niánjì xiǎo, **tǐlì yǒuxiàn**, suǒyǐ bǎ chūnyóu de zhǔyào huódòng dìng wéi zuò **yóulǎn chuán**. Yóulǎn chuán cóng Xīhú de dōngbiān kāi chuán, **shùn shízhēn fāngxiàng** yóu **biàn** Xīhú de nánbiān, xībiān hé běibiān, zuìhòu huí dào **zuìchū** de kāi chuán chù.

Considering that the students are young, and their **physical strength is limited**, the school decided to take the **excursion boat** as the main activity of the spring outing. The excursion boat sails from the east side of the West Lake, travels **clockwise** across the

south, west and north sides of West Lake, and finally returns to the **initial** sailing point.

对于老年人和小孩来说，在西湖坐游览船是很**流行**的。在**欣赏**西湖的美景的同时，他们还可以吃午餐和聊天儿。

Duìyú lǎonián rén hé xiǎohái lái shuō, zài Xīhú zuò yóulǎn chuán shì hěn **liúxíng** de. Zài xīnshǎng Xīhú de měijǐng de tóngshí, tāmen hái kěyǐ chī wǔcān hé liáotiānr.

With the elderly and children, it is very **popular** to take an excursion boat on West Lake. They can also have lunch and chat while **appreciating** the beautiful view of West Lake.

西湖很大，等游览船回到东边时，已经是下午三点半了。四个小时**不知不觉**地就过去了。

Xīhú hěn dà, děng yóulǎn chuán huí dào dōngbian shí, yǐjīng shì xiàwǔ sān diǎn bàn le. Sì gè xiǎoshí **bùzhī-bùjué** de jiù guòqùle.

West Lake is very big, and when the cruise ship returned to the east, it was already 3:30 in the afternoon. Four hours went by **without noticing**.

学生们晚上到家时已经七点了！多么好玩儿的春游啊！

Xuéshēngmen wǎnshang dào jiā shí yǐjīng qī diǎn le! Duōme hǎo wánr de chūnyóu a!

It was seven o'clock when the students got home at night! What a fun spring outing!

总结/Summary

约翰逊的小学每年都组织春游。今年他们去杭州西湖。学生和老师们是坐高铁从上海到杭州的。在杭州下了高铁后，他们直接坐了一辆旅游大客车到了西湖。学校考虑到学生们年纪小，体力有限，就安排学生和老师们坐了游览船。游览船从西湖的东边开船，顺时针方向游遍西湖的南边、西边和北边，最后回到最初的开船处。学生们在欣赏西湖美景的同时还可以聊天和吃午饭。几个小时很快就过去了。晚上学生们回到家时，已经快七点了！

Yuēhànxùn de xiǎoxué měi nián dōu zǔzhī chūnyóu. Jīnnián tāmen qù Hángzhōu Xīhú. Hángzhōu Xīhú fēngjǐngqū shì Zhōngguó shí dà wénmíng fēngjǐng lǚyóu qū hé guójiā wǔ A jí lǚyóu jǐng qū. Xuéshēng hé lǎoshīmen shì zuò gāotiě cóng Shànghǎi dào Hángzhōu de. Zài Hángzhōu xiàle gāotiě hòu, tāmen zhíjiē zuòle yíliàng lǚyóu dà kèchē dàole Xīhú. Xuéxiào kǎolǜ dào xuéshēngmen niánjì xiǎo, tǐlì yǒuxiàn, jiù ānpái xuéshēng hé lǎoshīmen zuòle yóulǎn chuán. Yóulǎn chuán cóng Xīhú de dōngbiān kāi chuán, shùn shízhēn fāngxiàng yóu biàn Xīhú de nánbiān, xībiān hé běibiān, zuìhòu huí dào zuìchū de kāi chuán chù. Xuéshēngmen zài xīnshǎng Xīhú měijǐng de tóngshí hái kěyǐ liáotiān hé chī wǔfàn. Jǐ gè xiǎoshí hěn kuài jiù guòqùle. Wǎnshang xuéshēngmen huí dào jiā shí, yǐjīng kuài qī diǎn le!

Johnson's primary school organizes a spring outing every year. This year they went to Hangzhou West Lake. Students and teachers take the high-speed train from Shanghai to Hangzhou. After getting off the high-speed rail in Hangzhou, they took a tourist bus directly to the West Lake. Considering that the students are young, and their physical strength is limited, the school arranged for the students and teachers to ride an excursion boat. The excursion boat sails from the east side of West Lake, travels clockwise around the south, west and north sides of West Lake, and finally returns to the initial sailing point. Students can chat and have lunch while appreciating the beautiful view of West Lake. Hours passed quickly. When the students returned home in the evening, it was seven o'clock!

生词/Vocabulary List

- 组织 – zǔzhī: to organize
- 春游 – chūnyóu: spring outing
- 立春 – lìchūn: beginning of spring
- 植物 – zhíwù: plant
- 发芽 – fāyá: to sprout
- 生长 – shēngzhǎng: to grow
- 鲜花 – xiānhuā: fresh flowers
- 开放 – kāifàng: to blossom
- 万物 – wànwù: all things
- 复苏 – fùsū: to revive
- 定 – dìng: to fix, to set
- 杭州 – Hángzhōu: Hangzhou
- 西湖 – Xīhú: West Lake
- 一日游 – yí rì yóu: day trip
- 等不及了 – děng bùjíle: can't wait anymore
- 往常 – wǎngcháng: usually
- 高铁站 – gāotiě zhàn: high speed rail station
- 排好队 – pái hǎo duì: line up
- 秩序 – zhìxù: orderly manner
- 背上 – bèi shàng: on the back

- 背 – bēi: to carry on back
- 旅行包 – lǚxíng bāo: travel bag
- 装满 – zhuāng mǎn: to be full
- 必备品 – bì bèi pǐn: essentials
- 新 – xīn: new
- 座位 – zuòwèi: seat
- 软 – ruǎn: soft
- 舒服 – shūfu: comfortable
- 时速 – shísù: speed
- 公里 – gōnglǐ: kilometer
- 车厢 – chēxiāng: carriage
- 超静音 – chāo jìngyīn: ultra-quiet
- 到达 – dàodá: to arrive
- 出口 – chūkǒu: exit
- 直接 – zhíjiē: immediate, direct
- 安排 – ānpái: to arrange
- 大客车 – dà kèchē: coach
- 目的地 – mùdìdì: destination
- 考虑 – kǎolǜ: to consider
- 体力 – tǐlì: physical strength
- 有限 – yǒuxiàn: limited

- 游览船 – yóulǎn chuán: excursion boat
- 顺时针 – shùn shízhēn: clockwise
- 方向 – fāngxiàng: direction
- 遍 – biàn: all over
- 最初 – zuìchū: original, initial
- 流行 – liúxíng: popular
- 欣赏 – xīnshǎng: to appreciate, to enjoy
- 不知不觉 – bùzhī-bùjué: without noticing

问题/Questions

1. 约翰逊的小学不是每年都组织春游。

   Johnson's primary school does not organize spring outings every year.

   A. 对
   B. 错

2. 在春游当天，学生们还像往常一样去了小学。

   On the day of the spring outing, the students went to the primary school as usual.

   A. 对
   B. 错

3. 学生们是怎么样从上海到杭州的？

   How did the students go from Shanghai to Hangzhou?

   A. 坐火车
   B. 坐汽车
   C. 坐高铁
   D. 骑自行车

4. 由于学生们年纪小，体力有限，所以他们坐了游览船。

   Since the students were young and had limited physical strength, they took the excursion boat.

   A. 对
   B. 错

5. 学生们是几点回到家的？

   What time did the students return to Shanghai in the evening?

   A. 下午四点
   B. 下午五点
   C. 晚上六点
   D. 晚上七点

答案/Answers

1. B 错
   False

2. A 对
   True

3. C 坐高铁
   Take high-speed train

4. A 对
   True

5. D 晚上七点
   Seven o'clock in the evening

CHAPTER 5

到东南亚度假 –
VACATION TO SOUTHEAST ASIA

一年一度的**暑假**又到了！今年暑假约翰逊要和爸爸妈妈一起到**东南亚玩一圈**。

过去的三年，由于**新冠肺炎**的原因，约翰逊一家没能**出国度假**，现在**一切都过去了**，大家又开始出国，到处看看玩玩。

约翰逊一家**打算**要去三个**国家**，它们**分别**是：**泰国、新加坡和马来西亚**。约翰逊的爸爸妈妈计划在东南亚一共呆**五个星期**：新加坡一个星期，马来西亚两个星期，泰国两个星期。

新加坡是东南亚的一个小**岛国**，**居民以华人、马来人和印度人为主**。**官方语言**有英文、中文、马来文和**泰米尔文**。新加坡是**公认**的**美食天堂**，受到几种不同饮食文化的**影响**，**融合交汇**出了新加坡的**独有味道**。新加坡市有**"花园城市"**之称，是**世界**上最大**港口**之一和**重要**的国际**金融**中心。

泰国是东南亚的旅游**胜地**。泰国的**气候适宜**，每年的 11 月份到第二年的 2 月份是泰国旅游的**最佳**时间。泰国还有很多的**传统**文化节日，比如说：**水灯节、守夏节和佛教节**等等。泰国以这些传统的节日**资源**，**吸引**了不少的世界**各地**的**游客**前来**游玩**。泰国还有漂亮和**干净**的**沙滩**。这次约翰逊一家就是去有名的**普吉岛**。

马来西亚是东南亚的一个大国。约翰逊的爸爸大学**毕业**后在**吉隆坡教**过两年英语，所以这次约翰逊一家会在吉隆坡呆一个星期，看看约翰逊爸爸的一些老朋友。约翰逊的妈妈一直都想去**槟城**看看。她听说槟城有很多**佛教**的**寺庙**和不同文化的**艺术街区**。她已经期盼很**久**了！

到东南亚度假 – Vacation to Southeast Asia
With English Translation

一年一度的**暑假**又到了！今年暑假约翰逊要和爸爸妈妈一起到**东南亚**玩一**圈**。

Yì nián yí dù de **shǔjià** yòu dàole! Jīnnián shǔjià Yuēhànxùn yào hé bàba māma yìqǐ dào **Dōngnányà** wán yì **quān**.

The **annual summer vacation** is here again! This summer, Johnson will go to **Southeast Asia** with his parents for vacation.

过去的三年，**由于新冠肺炎**的原因，约翰逊一家没能**出国度假**，现在**一切**都过去了，大家又开始出国，到处看看玩玩。

Guòqù de sān nián, **yóuyú xīnguān fèiyán** de yuányīn, Yuēhànxùn yì jiā méi néng **chūguó dùjià**, xiànzài **yíqiè** dōu guòqùle, dàjiā yòu kāishǐ chūguó, dàochù kànkan wán wan.

For the **past** three years, due to **COVID-19**, the Johnson family has not been able to **go abroad for vacation**. Now that **everything** is over, everyone is going abroad again to visit different places.

约翰逊一家**打算**要去三个**国家**，它们**分别**是：**泰国、新加坡和马来西亚**。约翰逊的爸爸妈妈计划在东南亚一共呆五个星期：新加坡一个星期，马来西亚两个星期，泰国两个星期。

Yuēhànxùn yì jiā **dǎsuàn** yào qù sān gè **guójiā**, tāmen **fēnbié** shì: **Tàiguó, Xīnjiāpō** hé **Mǎláixīyà**. Yuēhànxùn de bàba māma jìhuà zài Dōngnányà **yígòng dāi** wǔ gè xīngqī: Xīnjiāpō yígè xīngqī, Mǎláixīyà liǎnggè xīngqī, Tàiguó liǎnggè xīngqī.

The Johnson family **plans** to go to three **countries**: **Thailand**, **Singapore** and **Malaysia**. Johnson's parents plan to **spend a total of** five weeks in Southeast Asia: One week in Singapore, two weeks in Malaysia, and two weeks in Thailand.

新加坡是东南亚的一个小岛国，居民以华人、马来人和印度人为主。官方语言有英文、中文、马来文和泰米尔文。

Xīnjiāpō shì Dōngnányà de yígè xiǎo dǎoguó, **jūmín yǐ huárén**, **mǎ lái rén** hé yìndù rén **wéi zhǔ**. **Guānfāng yǔyán** yǒu Yīngwén, Zhōngwén, Mǎláiwén hé **Tàimǐ'ěrwén**.

Singapore is a small **island** country in Southeast Asia, and its **residents** are **mainly Chinese, Malays** and Indians. The **official languages** are English, Chinese, Malay and **Tamil**.

新加坡是公认的美食天堂。受到几种不同饮食文化的影响，融合交汇出了新加坡的独有味道。新加坡市有"花园城市"之称，是世界上最大港口之一和重要的国际金融中心。

Xīnjiāpō shì **gōngrèn** de **měishí tiāntáng**. **Shòu dào** jǐ zhǒng bùtóng yǐnshí wénhuà de **yǐngxiǎng**, **rónghé jiāohuì** chūle Xīnjiāpō de **dú yǒu wèidào**. Xīnjiāpō Shì yǒu "**huāyuán chéngshì**" zhī **chēng**, shì **shìjiè** shàng zuìdà **gǎngkǒu zhī yī** hé **zhòngyào** de guójì **jīnróng** zhōngxīn.

Singapore is **recognized** as a **foodie paradise**. **Influenced** by several different food cultures, the **fusion** brings together the **unique taste** of Singapore. Known as the "**Garden City**", Singapore is **one of** the largest **ports** in the **world** and an **important** international **financial** center.

泰国是东南亚的旅游胜地。泰国的气候适宜，每年的 11 月份到第二年的 2 月份是泰国旅游的最佳时间。

Tàiguó shì Dōngnányà de lǚyóu **shèngdì**. Tàiguó de **qìhòu shìyí**, měi nián de 11 yuèfèn dào dì èr nián de 2 yuèfèn shì Tàiguó lǚyóu de **zuì jiā** shíjiān.

Thailand is a tourist **destination** in Southeast Asia. Thailand has a **good climate**, and the **best time** to travel in Thailand is from November to February.

泰国还有很多的**传统文化节日**，比如说：**水灯节、守夏节和佛教节**等等。泰国以这些传统的节日**资源**，**吸引**了不少的世界**各地**的**游客**前来**游玩**。

Tàiguó hái yǒu hěnduō de **chuántǒng** wénhuà **jiérì**, bǐrú shuō: **Shuǐdēngjié, Shǒuxiàjié** hé **Fójiàojié** děng děng. Tàiguó yǐ zhèxiē chuántǒng de jiérì **zīyuán**, **xīyǐn** le bù shǎo de shìjiè **gèdì** de **yóukè** qián lái **yóuwán**.

There are also many **traditional** cultural **festivals** in Thailand, such as **Loy Krathong Festival, Buddhist Lent Day, Buddhist Festival**. With these traditional festival **resources**, Thailand has **attracted** many **tourists** from **every part** of the world to come to Thailand **for holidays**.

泰国还有漂亮和**干净**的**沙滩**。这次约翰逊一家就是去有名的**普吉岛**。

Tàiguó hái yǒu piàoliang hé **gānjìng** de **shātān**. Zhè cì Yuēhànxùn yìjiā jiùshì qù yǒumíng de **Pǔjídǎo**.

Thailand also has beautiful and **clean beaches**. This time the Johnson family is going to the famous **Phuket Island**.

马来西亚是东南亚的一个大国。约翰逊的爸爸大学**毕业**后在**吉隆坡教**过两年英语，所以这次约翰逊一家会在吉隆坡呆一个星期，看看约翰逊爸爸的一些老朋友。

Mǎláixīyà shì Dōngnányà de yígè dàguó. Yuēhànxùn de bàba dàxué **bìyè** hòu zài **Jílóngpō** jiāo guò liǎng nián Yīngyǔ, suǒyǐ zhè cì Yuēhànxùn yìjiā huì zài Jílóngpō dāi yígè xīngqī, kàn kan Yuēhànxùn bàba de yìxiē lǎo péngyǒu.

Malaysia is a large country in Southeast Asia. Johnson's father **taught** English in **Kuala Lumpur** for two years after **graduating** from university, so this time the Johnson family will stay in Kuala Lumpur for a week to see some old friends of Johnson's father.

约翰逊的妈妈一直都想去**槟城**看看。她听说槟城有很多佛教的**寺庙**和不同文化的**艺术街区**。她已经期盼很**久**了！

Yuēhànxùn de māma yìzhí dōu xiǎng qù **Bīnchéng** kànkan. Tā tīng shuō Bīnchéng yǒu hěnduō fójiào de **sìmiào** hé bùtóng wénhuà de **yìshù jiēqū**. Tā yǐjīng qí pàn hěn**jiǔ**le!

Johnson's mother has always wanted to visit **Penang**. She heard that Penang has many Buddhist **temples** and **art districts** with different cultures. She has been looking forward to it **for a long time**!

总结/Summary

今年暑假约翰逊的一家要去东南亚的新加坡、泰国和马来西亚旅游。过去的两三年，由于新冠肺炎的原因，他们一家没有出国旅游，现在一切都过去了，他们又可以出国到处看一看玩一玩。他们的假期一共五个星期。一个星期在新加坡，两个星期在泰国，最后两个星期在马来西亚。新加坡是一个很漂亮的东南亚岛国，有'花园城市'之称。泰国是东南亚的旅游胜地，它的气候适宜，有漂亮和干净的沙滩。约翰逊一家这次就是去有名的普吉岛。泰国还有很多传统的文化节日，比如说：水灯节、守夏节和佛教节等等。在马来西亚，他们要去吉隆坡看约翰逊爸爸的一些老朋友，还要去槟城看看。

Jīnnián shǔjià Yuēhànxùn de yìjiā yào qù Dōngnányà de Xīnjiāpō, Tàiguó hé Mǎláixīyà lǚyóu. Guòqù de liǎng sān nián, yóuyú xīnguān fèiyán de yuányīn, tāmen yìjiā méiyǒu chūguó lǚyóu, xiànzài yíqiè dōu guòqùle, tāmen yòu kěyǐ chūguó dàochù kàn yi kàn wán yi wán. Tāmen de jiàqī yígòng wǔ gè xīngqī. Yígè xīngqī zài Xīnjiāpō, liǎng gè xīngqī zài Tàiguó, zuìhòu liǎng gè xīngqī zài Mǎláixīyà. Xīnjiāpō shì yígè hěn piàoliang de Dōngnányà dǎoguó, yǒu 'huāyuán chéngshì' zhī chēng. Tàiguó shì Dōngnányà de lǚyóu shèngdì, tā de qìhòu shìyí, yǒu piàoliang hé gānjìng de shātān. Yuēhànxùn yìjiā zhè cì jiùshì qù yǒumíng de Pǔjídǎo. Tàiguó hái yǒu hěnduō chuántǒng de wénhuà jiérì, bǐrú shuō: Shuǐdēngjié, Shǒuxiàjié hé Fójiàojié děng děng. Zài Mǎláixīyà, tāmen yào qù Jílóngpō kàn Yuēhànxùn bàba de yìxiē lǎo péngyǒu, hái yào qù Bīnchéng kàn kan.

This summer, Johnson's family will travel to Singapore, Thailand and Malaysia in Southeast Asia. In the past two to three years, due to COVID-19, their family has not traveled abroad. Now that everything has passed, they can go abroad to sightsee again. Their vacation is five weeks in total. One week in Singapore, two weeks in Thailand and the last two weeks in Malaysia. Singapore is a beautiful island country in Southeast Asia, known as the "Garden City". Thailand is a tourist destination in Southeast Asia; it has a good climate, beautiful and clean sandy beaches. The Johnson family is going to the famous Phuket this time. Thailand also has many traditional cultural festivals, such as: Loy Krathong, Buddhist Lent Day and Buddhist Festival, etc. In Malaysia, they're going to Kuala Lumpur to see some old friends of Johnson's dad, and to Penang.

生词/Vocabulary List

- 一年一度 – yì nián yí dù: annual
- 暑假 – shǔjià: summer holiday
- 东南亚 – Dōngnányà: Southeast Asia
- 圈 – quān: measure word used with verb, meaning circle
- 过去 – guòqù: previous, former
- 由于 – yóuyú: because of, due to, owing to
- 新冠肺炎 – xīnguān fèiyán: COVID-19
- 出国 – chūguó: go abroad
- 度假 – dùjià: to go on holiday, to be on vacation
- 一切 – yíqiè: everything, all
- 打算 – dǎsuàn: to plan, to intend
- 国家 – guójiā: nation
- 分别 – fēnbié: respectively
- 泰国 – Tàiguó : Thailand
- 新加坡 – Xīnjiāpō: Singapore
- 马来西亚 – Mǎláixīyà: Malaysia

- 一共 – yígòng: total, altogether
- 呆 – dāi: to stay
- 岛 – dǎo: island
- 居民 – jūmín: resident
- 以...为主 – yǐ...wéi zhǔ: to be mainly of
- 华人 – huárén: Chinese
- 马来人 – mǎ lái rén: Malay
- 官方 – guānfāng: official
- 语言 – yǔyán: language
- 泰米尔文 – Tàimǐ'ěrwén: Tamil
- 公认 – gōngrèn: generally acknowledged, publicly known
- 美食 – měishí: delicious food
- 天堂 – tiāntáng: heaven
- 受到 – shòu dào: received
- 影响 – yǐngxiǎng: influence
- 融合 – rónghé: to mix together, to merge, fusion
- 交汇 – jiāohuì: to meet, to join
- 独有 – dú yǒu: unique
- 味道 – wèidào: taste, flavor

- 花园城市 – huāyuán chéngshì: Garden City
- 之称– zhī chēng: called
- 世界 – shìjiè: world
- 港口 – gǎngkǒu: port
- 之一 – zhī yī: one of
- 重要 – zhòngyào: important
- 金融 – jīnróng: finance
- 胜地 – shèngdì: well-known place
- 气候 – qìhòu: climate
- 适宜 – shìyí: good, suitable
- 最佳 – zuì jiā: optimal
- 传统 – chuántǒng: tradition
- 节日 – jiérì: festival
- 水灯节 – Shuǐdēngjié: Loy Krathong
- 守夏节 – Shǒuxià jié: summer festival
- 佛教节 – Fójiàojié: Buddhist festival
- 资源 – zīyuán: resource
- 吸引 – xīyǐn: absorb
- 各地 – gè dì: everywhere
- 游客 – yóukè: tourists
- 游玩 – yóuwán: to go sightseeing
- 干净 – gānjìng: clean
- 沙滩 – shātān: beach
- 毕业 – bìyè, to graduate
- 吉隆坡 – Jílóngpō, Kuala Lumpur
- 教 – jiāo: to teach
- 寺庙 – sìmiào, temple
- 艺术 – yìshù, art
- 街区 – jiēqū, block, district

问题/Questions

1. 过去的两三年，约翰逊一家每年都出国旅游。

   For the past two to three years, the Johnson family have traveled abroad every year.

   A. 对
   B. 错

2. 约翰逊一家今年暑假要去东南亚的三个国家。

   The Johnson family is going to three countries in Southeast Asia this summer.

   A. 对
   B. 错

3. 他们都要去哪几个国家？

   Which countries are they going to?

   A. 泰国、新加坡、马来西亚
   B. 泰国、马来西亚、柬埔寨
   C. 新加坡、马来西亚、菲律宾
   D. 英国、泰国、新加坡

4. 在泰国，约翰逊一家要去哪里玩？

   Where are the Johnson family going to visit in Thailand?

   A. 吉隆坡
   B. 槟城
   C. 普吉岛
   D. 曼谷

5. 约翰逊一家为什么要去吉隆坡？

   Why does the Johnson family want to go to Kuala Lumpur?

   A. 去吃美食。
   B. 去看约翰逊爸爸的老朋友。
   C. 去看艺术街区。
   D. 因为吉隆坡气候很好。

答案/Answers

1. B 错

   False

2. A 对

   True

3. A 泰国、新加坡、马来西亚

   Thailand, Singapore, Malaysia

4. C 普吉岛

   Phuket

5. B 去看约翰逊爸爸的老朋友。

   To go to see old friends of Johnson's dad.

CHAPTER 6
卖旧家具– SELLING OLD FURNITURE

住在德国**慕尼黑**的桑德拉今年**初**找到了**一份**新工作，**薪水**也**涨**了。

六月底的时候她**如愿以偿**地买了一张新床和一些新的**家具**。她把家里**客厅**和**卧室**的墙

也**重新刷**了一遍。旧家变成了新家。

现在她需要把她的旧床和旧家具卖掉。她只有一个月的时间，因为一个月以后她妈妈要从德国南部来慕尼黑看她，桑德拉不想家里那时**到处**还**堆**着旧家具，她想让妈妈看到她漂亮的新家。

她问了问她几个**年轻**的**同事怎么样**可以尽**快**而且**高价**地卖掉这些旧家具。他们建议了几个 **App** 和慕尼黑**当地的二手市场**。

桑德拉的第一个选择是**脸书**的二手市场。脸书是在 2016 年**推出**这个新的**交易平台**的。几年时间，这个平台发展成了一个和**易趣**一样流行的**个人**和**商务**交易平台。脸书是全世界最大的个人**社交媒体**。桑德拉当然也有脸书的个人**账户**了。她花了一两个小时的时间给旧家具拍了照片，在平台上写了一些**关于**旧家具的**简单介绍**，就把全部要卖的旧家具放到脸书的市场上了。**接下来**的几天，有很多人**联系**了桑德拉，问了一些关于几件旧家具的**问题**。当**然了，对**他们**感兴趣**的家具，**大多数**的人都问桑德拉能不能**便宜**一点。桑德拉也是一个**很好说话**的人，没有几天的时间大多数的旧家具就被人买走了，**剩下的**只有两个**镜子**和一些小的**装饰品**。

慕尼黑当地有一个很大的**跳蚤**市场。桑德拉以前和朋友一起去过几次。跳蚤市场**附近**有一间桑德拉最喜欢的咖啡店。这个星期天桑德拉准备早早起床到跳蚤市场找一个**热闹**的**角落**，试着卖掉最后的几件小东西，然后到她最喜欢的咖啡店喝一杯热咖啡。

星期天早上十点，桑德拉找到了一个热闹的角落，把要卖的东西也全部**摆好**了，只**等**着**买家光顾**了！可是大半个上午过去了，只有一对老**夫妇**和一个年轻的男孩看了看桑德拉的要

卖的镜子和几件小的装饰品，他们看起来不是很感兴趣，**连价钱**也没有问。下午的时候**竟然**下起了雨，桑德拉**急急忙忙**地把东西全部**收起来**，**飞快**地坐进了车里。半个小时过去了，雨一点儿也没有要**停**的**意思**。桑德拉**无意间**看见在对面的街上有一家开着门的**慈善**商店。桑德拉想了两分钟，决定把没有卖掉的东西**捐献**给**对面**的慈善商店。

十分钟以后，桑德拉在她最爱的咖啡馆一边听着**爵士乐**，一边喝着热咖啡。

星期天**终于**到了！

卖旧家具 – Selling Old Furniture
With English Translation

住在德国**慕尼黑**的桑德拉今年**初**找到了一**份**新工作，**薪水**也**涨**了。

Zhù zài Déguó **Mùníhēi** de Sāngdélā jīnnián **chū** zhǎodàole yífèn xīn gōngzuò, **xīnshuǐ** yě **zhǎng**le.

Sandra, who lives in **Munich**, Germany, found **a** new job at the **beginning** of this year. Her **salary** also **increased**.

六月底的时候她**如愿以偿**地买了一张新床和一些新的**家具**。她把家里**客厅**和**卧室的墙**

也**重新刷**了一**遍**。旧家变成了新家。

Liù yuè dǐ de shíhou tā **rúyuànyǐcháng** de mǎile yìzhāng xīn chuáng hé yìxiē xīn de **jiājù**. Tā bǎ jiālǐ **kètīng** hé **wòshì** de **qiáng** yě **chóngxīn shuā**le **yíbiàn**. Jiùjiā biàn chéngle xīnjiā.

At the end of June, she **fulfilled her wish** and bought a new bed and some new **furniture**. She also **repainted** the **walls** of the **living room** and **bedroom**. The **old** home became the new home.

现在她需要把她的旧床和旧家具卖掉。她只有一个月的时间，因为一个月以后她妈妈要从德国南部来慕尼黑看她，桑德拉不想家里那时**到处**还**堆**着旧家具，她想让妈妈看到她漂亮的新家。

Xiànzài tā xūyào bǎ tā de jiù chuáng hé jiù jiājù mài diào. Tā zhǐyǒu yígè yuè de shíjiān, yīnwèi yígè yuè yǐhòu tā māma yào cóng Déguó nánbù lái Mùníhēi kàn tā, Sāngdélā bù xiǎng jiālǐ nà shí **dàochù** hái **duī**zhe jiù jiājù, tā xiǎng ràng māma kàn dào tā piàoliang de xīnjiā.

Now she needs to sell her old bed and old furniture. She only has one month, because in a month her mother will come to Munich from the south of Germany to visit her. Sandra doesn't want the house to be still **piled up** with old furniture **everywhere** at that time. She wants her mother to see her beautiful new home.

她问了问她几个**年轻**的**同事怎么样**可以尽快而且**高价**地卖掉这些旧家具。他们建议了几个 **App** 和慕尼黑当地的**二手市场**。

Tā wènle wèn tā jǐ gè **niánqīng** de **tóngshì zěnme yàng** kěyǐ **jǐnkuài** érqiě **gāojià** de mài diào zhèxiē jiù jiājù. Tāmen jiànyìle jǐ gè **App** hé Mùníhēi **dāngdì** de **èrshǒu shìchǎng**.

She asked several of her **young colleagues how** she could sell the old furniture **quickly** and at **a high price**. They suggested several **apps** and a **local second-hand market** in Munich.

桑德拉的第一个选择是**脸书**的二手市场。脸书是在 2016 年**推出**这个新的**交易平台**的。几年时间，这个平台发展成了一个和**易趣**一样流行的**个人**和**商务**交易平台。脸书是全世界最大的个人**社交媒体**。

Sāngdélā de dìyī gè xuǎnzé shì **Liǎnshū** de èrshǒu shìchǎng. Liǎnshū shì zài 2016 nián **tuīchū** zhège xīn de **jiāoyì píngtái** de. Jǐ nián shíjiān, zhège píngtái fāzhǎn chéngle yí gè hé **Yìqù** yíyàng liúxíng de **gèrén** hé **shāngwù** jiāoyì píngtái. Liǎnshū shì quán shìjiè zuìdà de gèrén **shèjiāo méitǐ**.

Sandra's first choice was **Facebook**'s secondhand market. Facebook **launched** this new **trading platform** in 2016. In a few years, the platform developed into a platform as popular as **eBay** for **personal** and **business** transactions. Facebook is the largest personal **social media** platform in the world.

桑德拉当然也有脸书的个人**账户**了。她花了一两个小时的时间给旧家具拍了照片，在平台上写了一些**关于**旧家具的**简单介绍**，就把全部要卖的旧家具放到脸书的市场上了。

Sāngdélā dāngrán yě yǒu Liǎnshū de gèrén **zhànghù**le. Tā huāle yì liǎng gè xiǎoshí de shíjiān gěi jiù jiājù pāile zhàopiàn, zài píngtái shàng xiěle yìxiē **guānyú** jiù jiājù de **jiǎndān jièshào**, jiù bǎ quánbù yào mài de jiù jiājù fàng dào Liǎnshū de shìchǎng shàng le.

Sandra, of course, also has a personal Facebook **account**. She spent an hour or two taking pictures of the old furniture, wrote some **brief introductions about** the old furniture on the platform, and put all the old furniture for sale on the Facebook marketplace.

接下来的几天，有很多人联系了桑德拉，问了一些关于几件旧家具的问题。当然了，对他们感兴趣的家具，大多数的人都问桑德拉能不能便宜一点。

Jiē xiàlái de jǐ tiān, yǒu hěnduō rén **liánxì**le Sāngdélā, wènle yìxiē guānyú jǐ jiàn jiù jiājù de **wèntí. Dāngránle,** duì tāmen **gǎn xìngqù** de jiājù, **dàduōshù** de rén dōu wèn Sāngdélā néng bùnéng **piányi** yīdiǎn.

Over the **following** few days, Sandra was **contacted** by many people with **questions** about several pieces of the old furniture. **Of course**, the **majority of the people** asked Sandra if the prices could be **cheaper** for the furniture items they were interested in.

桑德拉也是一个**很好说话**的人，没有几天的时间大多数的旧家具就被人买走了，**剩下的**只有两个**镜子**和一些小的**装饰品**。

Sāngdélā yě shì yígè **hěn hǎo shuōhuà** de rén, méiyǒu jǐ tiān de shíjiān dà duō shù de jiù jiājù jiù bèi rén mǎi zǒule, **shèng xià de** zhǐyǒu liǎng gè **jìngzi** hé yìxiē xiǎo de **zhuāngshì pǐn.**

Sandra is a person who is very **easy to talk to.** Within a few days most of the old furniture was bought, with only two **mirrors** and a few small **ornaments left.**

慕尼黑当地有一个很大的**跳蚤**市场。桑德拉以前和朋友一起去过几次。跳蚤市场**附近**有一间桑德拉最喜欢的咖啡店。

Mùníhēi dāngdì yǒu yígè hěn dà de **tiàozǎo** shìchǎng. Sāngdélā yǐqián hé péngyǒu yìqǐ qù guò jǐ cì. Tiàozǎo shìchǎng **fùjìn** yǒu yìjiàn Sāngdélā zuì xǐhuān de kāfēi diàn.

There is a big **flea** market in Munich. Sandra has been there a few times before with friends. Sandra's favorite coffee shop is **close to** the flea market.

这个星期天桑德拉准备早早起床到跳蚤市场找一个**热闹**的**角落**，试着卖掉最后的几件小东西，然后到她最喜欢的咖啡店喝一杯热咖啡。

Zhège xīngqītiān Sāngdélā zhǔnbèi zǎozǎo qǐchuáng dào tiàozǎo shìchǎng zhǎo yígè **rènào** de **jiǎoluò**, shìzhe mài diào zuìhòu de jǐ jiàn xiǎo dōngxi, ránhòu dào tā zuì xǐhuān de kāfēi diàn hè yìbēi rè kāfēi.

This Sunday Sandra is going to get up early to find a **bustling corner** in the flea market, try to sell the last few little things, and then stop by her favorite coffee shop for a hot cup of coffee.

星期天早上十点，桑德拉找到了一个热闹的角落，把要卖的东西也全部**摆好**了，只**等**着**买家光顾**了！

Xīngqītiān zǎoshang shí diǎn, Sāngdélā zhǎodàole yígè rènào de jiǎoluò, bǎ yào mài de dōngxi yě quánbù **bǎihǎo**le, zhǐ **děng**zhe **mǎi jiā guānggù**le!

At ten o'clock Sunday morning, Sandra found a bustling corner and **displayed** all the things for sale, just **waiting** for **buyers** to **pay a visit**.

可是大半个上午过去了，只有一对老**夫妇**和一个年轻的男孩看了看桑德拉的要卖的镜子和几件小的装饰品，他们看起来不是很感兴趣，**连价钱**也没有问。

Kěshì dà bàn gè shàngwǔ guòqùle, zhǐyǒu yí duì lǎo **fūfù** hé yígè niánqīng de nánhái kànle kàn Sāngdélā de yāo mài de jìngzi hé jǐ jiàn xiǎo de zhuāngshì pǐn, tāmen kàn qǐlái bú shì hěn gǎn xìngqù, lián **jiàqián** yě méiyǒu wèn.

But most of the morning went by, and then there were only an old **couple** and a young boy looking at Sandra's mirror and a few small decorations. They didn't seem very interested and didn't **even** ask for the **price**.

下午的时候**竟然**下起了雨，桑德拉**急急忙忙**地把东西全部**收起来**，飞**快**地坐进了车里。半个小时过去了，雨一点儿也没有要**停**的**意思**。

Xiàwǔ de **shíhou** jìngrán xià qǐle yǔ, Sāngdélā **jíjí-mángmáng** de bǎ dōngxi quánbù **shōu qǐlái**, **fēikuài** de zuò jìnle chē lǐ. Bàn gè xiǎoshí guòqùle, yǔ yìdiǎnr yě méiyǒu yào **tíng** de yìsi.

It started to rain **unexpectedly** in the afternoon. Sandra **collected** everything and got into the car **rapidly**. Half an hour passed, and the rain had no **intention** of **stopping** at all.

桑德拉**无意间**看见在对面的街上有一家开着门的**慈善**商店。桑德拉想了两分钟，决定把没有卖掉的东西**捐献**给**对面**的慈善商店。

Sāngdélā **wúyì jiān** kànjiàn zài duìmiàn de jiē shàng yǒu yìjiā kāizhe mén de **císhàn** shāngdiàn. Sāngdélā xiǎngle liǎng fēnzhōng, juédìng bǎ méiyǒu mài diào de dōngxi **juānxiàn** gěi **duìmiàn** de císhàn shāngdiàn.

Sandra **happened to** see a **charity** shop that was open across the street. Sandra thought for two minutes and decided to **donate** what she didn't sell to the charity shop **opposite**.

十分钟以后，桑德拉在她最爱的咖啡馆一边听着**爵士乐**，一边喝着热咖啡。

Shí fēnzhōng yǐhòu, Sāngdélā zài tā zuì ài de kāfēi guǎn yìbiān tīngzhe **juéshìyuè**, yìbiān hē zhe rè kāfēi.

Ten minutes later, Sandra was in her favorite café listening to **jazz** while drinking hot coffee.

星期天终于到了!

Xīngqītiān **zhōngyú** dàole!

Sunday was **finally** here!

总结/Summary

住在慕尼黑的桑德拉今年初找到了一份新工作，薪水也涨了。她如愿以偿地买了一张新床和一些新家具。她的妈妈一个月以后要从德国的南部来看她，所以在这一个月她需要卖掉所有的旧家具。她问了问几个年轻的同事，他们告诉了桑德拉脸书的二手市场和当地的跳蚤市场。桑德拉在脸书的二手市场上卖掉了大多数的旧家具，剩下的只有两个镜子和一些小装饰品。一个星期天，桑德拉早早地来到当地的跳蚤市场，找了一个热闹的角落，然后把要卖的东西全部摆好。谁知过了大半天也没有人感兴趣，下午竟然又下起了雨。桑德拉无意间看见一家慈善商店。把要卖的东西捐给了慈善商店以后，桑德拉来到她最喜欢的咖啡店喝起了一杯热咖啡。

Zhù zài Mùníhēi de Sāngdélā jīnnián chū zhǎodàole yífèn xīn gōngzuò, xīnshuǐ yě zhǎngle. Tā rúyuànyǐcháng de mǎile yìzhāng xīn chuáng hé yìxiē xīn jiājù. Tā de māma yígè yuè yǐhòu yào cóng Déguó de nánbù lái kàn tā, suǒyǐ zài zhè yígè yuè tā xūyào mài diào suǒyǒu de jiù jiājù. Tā wènle wèn jǐ gè niánqīng de tóngshì, tāmen gàosùle Sāngdélā Liǎnshū de èrshǒu shìchǎng hé dāngdì de tiàozǎo shìchǎng. Sāngdélā zài Liǎnshū de èrshǒu shìchǎng shàng mài diàole dà duō shǔ de jiù jiājù, shèng xià de zhǐyǒu liǎnggè jìngzi hé yìxiē xiǎo zhuāngshì pǐn. Yígè xīngqītiān, Sāngdélā zǎozǎo de lái dào dāngdì de tiàozǎo shìchǎng, zhǎole yígè rènào de jiǎoluò, ránhòu bǎ yào mài de dōngxi quánbù bǎi hǎo. Shéi zhī guòle dà bàntiān yě méiyǒu rén gǎn xìngqù, xiàwǔ jìngrán yòu xià qǐle yǔ. Sāngdélā wúyì jiān kànjiàn yìjiā císhàn shāngdiàn. Bǎ yào mài de dōngxi juān gěile císhàn shāngdiàn yǐhòu, Sāngdélā lái dào tā zuì xǐhuān de kāfēi diàn hē qǐle yìbēi rè kāfēi.

Sandra, who lives in Munich, found a new job earlier this year, with a salary increase. She fulfilled her wish and bought a new bed and some new furniture. Her mother will be visiting her from the south of Germany in a month, so she needs to sell all her old furniture during this month. She asked a few young colleagues, and they told Sandra about the secondhand market on Facebook and about the local flea market. Sandra sold most of the old furniture on Facebook's secondhand market, leaving only two mirrors and a few ornaments to be sold. One Sunday, Sandra went to the local flea market early, found a bustling corner, and laid out everything for sale. No one was interested after most of the day went by, and it started to rain in the afternoon. Sandra unexpectedly saw a charity shop. After donating what she was selling to the charity shop, Sandra stopped by her favorite coffee shop for a hot cup of coffee.

生词/Vocabulary List

- 份 – fèn: measure word for job
- 慕尼黑 – Mùníhēi: Munich
- 初 – chū: at the beginning
- 薪水 – xīnshuǐ: salary
- 张 – zhāng: measure word for bed
- 如愿以偿 – rúyuànyǐcháng: fulfill one's wish
- 家具 – jiājù: furniture
- 客厅 – kètīng: living room
- 卧室 – wòshì: bedroom
- 墙 – qiáng: wall
- 重新 – chóngxīn: again
- 刷 – shuā: to brush, to paint
- 一遍 – yíbiàn: measure word used with verb, meaning once
- 旧 – jiù: old
- 到处 – dàochù: everywhere
- 堆 – duī: to pile, pile
- 年轻 – niánqīng: young
- 同事 – tóngshì: colleague
- 怎么样 – zěnme yàng: how
- 尽快 – jǐnkuài: as soon as possible
- 高价 – gāojià: high price

- App – a-p-p: app
- 当地 – dāngdì: local
- 二手 – èrshǒu: secondhand
- 市场 – shìchǎng: market
- 脸书 – Liǎnshū: Facebook
- 推出 – tuīchū: roll out
- 交易 – jiāoyì: trade
- 平台 – píngtái: platform
- 易趣 – Yìqù: eBay
- 个人 – gèrén: personal
- 商务 – shāngwù: business
- 社交媒体 – shèjiāo méitǐ: social media
- 账户 – zhànghù: account
- 关于 – guānyú: about
- 简单 – jiǎndān: simple
- 介绍 – jièshào: introduction
- 接下来 – jiē xiàlái: following, next
- 联系 – liánxì: get in touch, contact
- 问题 – wèntí: question
- 当然了 – dāngránle: of course
- 对...感兴趣 – duì...gǎn xìngqù: to be interested in
- 大多数 – dàduōshù: majority

- 便宜 – piányi: cheap
- 好说话 – hǎo shuōhuà: easy to talk to
- 剩下的 – shèng xià de: remaining, leftover
- 镜子 – jìngzi: mirror
- 装饰品 – zhuāngshì pǐn: decoration; ornament
- 跳蚤 – tiàozǎo: flea
- 附近 – fùjìn: nearby, close to
- 热闹 – rènào: lively, bustling
- 角落 – jiǎoluò: corner
- 摆好 – bǎi hǎo: to display
- 等 – děng: to wait
- 买家 – mǎi jiā: buyer
- 光顾 – guānggù: to pay a visit
- 夫妇 – fūfù: married couple
- 连 – lián: even
- 价钱 – jiàqián: price
- 竟然 – jìngrán: unexpectedly
- 急急忙忙 – jíji-mángmang: in a hurry
- 收起来 – shōu qǐlái: to collect
- 飞快 – fēikuài: rapid
- 停 – tíng: to stop
- 意思 – yìsi: intention
- 无意间 – wúyì jiān: unexpectedly
- 慈善 – císhàn: charitable
- 捐献 – juānxiàn: to donate
- 对面 – duìmiàn: opposite
- 爵士乐 – juéshìyuè: jazz
- 终于 – zhōngyú: finally

问题/Questions

1. 今年年初，住在德国慕尼黑的桑德拉有了一份新工作。

   In the beginning of this year, Sandra, who lives in Munich, Germany, got a new job.

   A. 对
   B. 错

2. 桑德拉把所有的旧家具捐给了一家慈善商店。

   Sandra donated all the old furniture to a charity shop.

   A. 对
   B. 错

3. 桑德拉没有脸书的个人账户。

   Sandra doesn't have a Facebook personal account.

   A. 对
   B. 错

4. 桑德拉星期天总是去当地的跳蚤市场。

   Sandra always goes to the local flea market on Sundays.

   A. 对
   B. 错

5. 桑德拉最喜欢的咖啡店离当地的跳蚤市场很远。

   Sandra's favorite coffee shop is far from the local flea market.

   A. 对
   B. 错

答案/Answers

1. A 对
   True

2. B 错
   False

3. B 错
   False

4. B 错
   False

5. B 错
   False

CHAPTER 7

跑伦敦马拉松 –
RUN THE LONDON MARATHON

奥利今年四十岁了，可是他看起来很年轻，也就三十五吧！

奥利**平时**参加各种各样的运动，最喜欢的还**得**说是**打橄榄球**和**跑马拉松**。

奥利二十八岁的时候跑过一次马拉松。当时他年轻，也没花什么时间准备，在马拉松的两三个月前才开始**训练**，训练的时候也是**马马虎虎**。马拉松跑是跑完了，时间也不错，可是马拉松后的**整个星期**，奥利的**全身**都很**疼痛**，**尤其**是腿和脚，有三天他都不能走路，因为实在是太痛了。

这次奥利**吸取**了上次的经验，计划要好好地准备马拉松。他决定给自己九个月的时间。最近他也加入了他家附近的一个跑步**俱乐部**。俱乐部给**会员**提供一些关于跑马拉松的训练**信息**。奥利还有一个跑步**伙伴**。这个伙伴是他的高中同学，他们已经认识二十多年了。一个月两次，他们都会在公园儿见面，每次都跑个十公里八公里的。

奥利也知道，训练重要，**饮食营养**和**休息同样**重要。去年的时候，奥利**经人介绍**找到了一个**合拍**的**营养师**。头一个月，营养师让奥利把每天吃的食物都记录下来。奥利觉得很**麻烦**，也很**浪费**时间，但是奥利还是**老老实实**地听了营养师的话。食物**日记表明**奥利吃的**碳水化合物**比例太高，**蛋白质**太低。接下来的几个月，奥利**改变**了一些**坏**的饮食**习惯，提高**了蛋白质的**摄入量，**同时也**减少**了碳水化合物的摄入量。现在奥利的食物日记是**无可挑剔**了！

接下来的九个月，奥利**遵循**了跑马拉松的训练计划。每天每个星期每个月奥利都**百分之百**地完成了应该做的训练。在这九个月中，奥利是越跑越快，越快越想跑，训练进入了一个**良性循环**。在跑马拉松的那天，奥利很**轻松**地**越过**了**终点线**。这次的时间比上一次的减少了二十多分钟。

上一次跑马拉松的时候奥利二十八岁，今年奥利四十岁。

跑伦敦马拉松 – Run the London Marathon
With English Translation

奥利今年四十岁了，可是他看起来很年轻，也就三十五吧！

Àolì jīnnián sìshí suì le, kěshì tā kàn qǐlái hěn niánqīng, yě jiù sānshíwǔ ba!

Oli is forty years old this year, but he looks very young, like a thirty-five year-old!

奥利**平时**参加各种各样的运动，最喜欢的还**得**说是**打橄榄球**和**跑马拉松**。

Àolì **píngshí** cānjiā gè zhǒng gè yàng de yùndòng, zuì xǐhuān de hái **děi** shuō shì **dǎ gǎnlǎnqiú** hé **pǎo mǎlāsōng**.

Oli **usually** participates in various sports, and his favorites are to **play rugby** and **run marathons.**

奥利二十八岁的时候跑过一次马拉松。当时他年轻，也没花什么时间准备，在马拉松的两三个月前才开始**训练**，训练的时候也是**马马虎虎**。

Àolì èrshíbā suì de shíhou pǎoguò yícì mǎlāsōng. Dāngshí tā niánqīng, yě méi huā shénme shíjiān zhǔnbèi, zài mǎlāsōng de liǎng sān gè yuè qián cái kāishǐ **xùnliàn**, xùnliàn de shíhou yěshì **mǎmǎhūhū**.

Oli ran a marathon when he was twenty-eight. He was young at the time, and he didn't spend much time preparing. He only started **training** two or three months before the marathon, and his training was **not very serious.**

马拉松跑是跑完了，时间也不错，可是马拉松后的**整个**星期，奥利的**全身**都很**疼痛**，**尤其**是腿和脚，有三天他都不能走路，因为实在是太痛了。

Mǎlāsōng pǎo shì pǎo wánle, shíjiān yě búcuò, kěshì mǎlāsōng hòu de **zhěnggè** xīngqī, Àolì de **quánshēn** dōu hěn **téngtòng**, **yóuqí** shì tuǐ hé jiǎo, yǒu sān tiān tā dōu bùnéng zǒulù, yīnwèi shízài shì tài tòngle.

The marathon was completed and the time was good, but for the **entire** week after the marathon, Oli's **whole body** was **in pain**, **especially** his legs and feet. For three days, he couldn't walk because it was so painful.

这次奥利**吸取**了上次的经验，计划要好好地准备马拉松。他决定给自己九个月的时间。

Zhè cì Àolì **xīqǔ**le shàng cì de jīngyàn, jìhuà yào hǎohao de zhǔnbèi mǎlāsōng. Tā juédìng gěi zìjǐ jiǔ gè yuè de shíjiān.

This time, Oli **learned from** the previous experience and planned to be well-prepared for the marathon. He decided to give himself nine months.

最近他也加入了他家附近的一个跑步**俱乐部**。俱乐部给**会员**提供一些关于跑马拉松的训练**信息**。

Zuìjìn tā yě jiārùle tā jiā fùjìn de yígè pǎobù **jùlèbù**. Jùlèbù gěi **huìyuán** tígōng yìxiē guānyú pǎo mǎlāsōng de xùnliàn **xìnxī**.

He also recently joined a running **club** close to his home. The club provides **members** with training **information** for running a marathon.

奥利还有一个跑步**伙伴**。这个伙伴是他的高中同学，他们已经认识二十多年了。一个月两次，他们都会在公园儿见面，每次都跑个十公里八公里的。

Àolì hái yǒu yígè pǎobù **huǒbàn**. Zhège huǒbàn shì tā de gāozhōng tóngxué, tāmen yǐjīng rènshí èrshí duō nián le. Yígè yuè liǎng cì, tāmen dōu huì zài gōngyuánr jiànmiàn, měi cì dōu pǎo gè shí gōnglǐ bā gōnglǐ de.

Oli also has a running **buddy**. This partner was his high school classmate. They have known each other for over twenty years. They meet in the park twice a month, and each time they run 8 to 10 kilometers.

奥利也知道，训练重要，饮食**营养**和**休息同样**重要。去年的时候，奥利经人**介绍**找到了一个**合拍**的**营养师**。

Àolì yě zhīdào, xùnliàn zhòngyào, **yǐnshí yíngyǎng** hé **xiūxi tóngyàng** zhòngyào. Qùnián de shíhou, Àolì **jīng** rén **jièshào** zhǎodàole yígè **hépāi** de **yíngyǎng shī**.

Oli also knows that while training is important, **nutrition** and **rest** are **equally** important. Last year, Oli **was introduced** to a **nutritionist** that he **gets along with**.

头一个月，营养师让奥利把每天吃的食物都**记录**下来。奥利觉得很**麻烦**，也很**浪费**时间，但是奥利还是**老老实实**地听了营养师的话。食物日记表明奥利吃的**碳水化合物**比例太高，**蛋白质**太低。

Tóu yígè yuè, yíngyǎng shī ràng Àolì bǎ měitiān chī de shíwù dōu **jìlù** xiàlái. Àolì juéde hěn **máfan**, yě hěn **làngfèi** shíjiān, dànshì Àolì háishì **lǎolǎo-shíshí** de tīngle yíngyǎng shī de huà. Shíwù **rìjì** biǎomíng Àolì chī de **tànshuǐ huàhéwù** bǐlì tài gāo, **dànbáizhì** tài dī.

For the **first** month, the nutritionist asked Oli to **keep a log** of what he ate every day. Oli thought it was a **hassle** and a **waste** of time, but he followed the nutritionist's advice **strictly**. The food **diary** indicated that the ratio of **carbohydrates** that Oli ate was too high and the **proteins** were too low.

接下来的几个月，奥利**改变**了一些**坏**的饮食习**惯**，**提高**了蛋白质的**摄入量**，同时也**减少**了碳水化合物的摄入量。现在奥利的食物日记是**无可挑剔**了！

Jiē xiàlái de jǐ gè yuè, Àolì **gǎibiàn**le yìxiē **huài** de yǐnshí **xíguàn**, **tígāo**le dànbáizhì de **shè rù liàng**, tóngshí yě **jiǎnshǎo**le tànshuǐ huàhéwù de shè rù liàng. Xiànzài Àolì de shíwù rìjì shì **wú kě tiāoti** le!

Over the next few months, Oli **changed** some of his **bad** eating **habits**. He **increased** his protein **intake** while also **reducing** his carbohydrate intake. Now Oli's food diary is **impeccable**!

接下来的九个月，奥利**遵循**了跑马拉松的训练计划。每天每个星期每个月奥利都**百分之百**地完成了应该做的训练。

Jiē xiàlái de jiǔ gè yuè, Àolì **zūnxún**le pǎo mǎlāsōng de xùnliàn jìhuà. Měitiān měi gè xīngqī měi gè yuè Àolì dōu **bǎifēnzhībǎi** de wánchéngle yīnggāi zuò de xùnliàn.

Over the next nine months, Oli **followed** a training plan for running a marathon. Every day, every week, every month, Oli gave **100%** to the training he was supposed to do.

在这九个月中，奥利是越跑越快，越快越想跑，训练进入了一个**良性循环**。在跑马拉松的那天，奥利很**轻松**地**越过**了终点线。这次的时间比上一次的减少了二十多分钟。

Zài zhè jiǔ gè yuè zhōng, Àolì shì yuè pǎo yuè kuài, yuè kuài yuè xiǎng pǎo, xùnliàn jìnrùle yígè **liángxìng xúnhuán**. Zài pǎo mǎlāsōng de nàtiān, Àolì hěn **qīngsōng** de **yuèguò**le **zhōngdiǎn xiàn**. Zhè cì de shíjiān bǐ shàng yícì de jiǎnshǎole èrshí duō fēnzhōng.

In these nine months, Oli ran faster and faster, and the faster he ran, the more he would like to run; the training entered a **virtuous circle**. On the day of the marathon, Oli **crossed** the **finish line with ease**. His time for running this marathon was twenty minutes less than the last time.

上一次跑马拉松的时候奥利二十八岁，今年奥利四十岁。

Shàng yícì pǎo mǎlāsōng de shíhou Àolì èrshíbā suì, jīnnián Àolì sìshí suì.

Oli was twenty-eight years old when he last ran a marathon, and he is forty this year.

总结/Summary

奥利今年四十岁，他最喜欢的运动是打橄榄球和跑马拉松。他二十八岁的时候跑过一次马拉松。当时他很年轻，也没有怎么训练，可是跑完马拉松的整个星期，他的全身都很疼痛，有三天他都不能走路。这次他打算好好准备，他给了自己九个月的时间。他参加了他家附近的一个跑步俱乐部。他也知道，训练重要，饮食营养和休息一样重要。他经人介绍找到了一个很合拍的营养师。营养师让他把吃的所有东西都记录下来。接下来的几个月，奥利改变了一些坏的饮食习惯，在提高蛋白质摄入量的同时，也减少了碳水化合物的摄入量。奥利越跑越快，越快越想跑。这九个月的训练很成功。在跑马拉松的当天，他不但轻松地越过了终点线，而且用的时间也比二十八岁的那次马拉松少了很多。

Àolì jīnnián sìshí suì, tā zuì xǐhuān de yùndòng shì dǎ gǎnlǎnqiú hé pǎo mǎlāsōng. Tā èrshíbā suì de shíhou pǎo guò yícì mǎlāsōng. Dāngshí tā hěn niánqīng, yě méiyǒu zěnme xùnliàn, kěshì pǎo wán mǎlāsōng de zhěnggè xīngqī, tā de quánshēn dōu hěn téngtòng, yǒu sān tiān tā dōu bùnéng zǒulù. Zhè cì tā dǎsuàn hǎohao zhǔnbèi, tā gěile zìjǐ jiǔ gè yuè de shíjiān. Tā cānjiāle tā jiā fùjìn de yígè pǎobù jùlèbù. Tā yě zhīdào, xùnliàn zhòngyào, yǐnshí yíngyǎng hé xiūxi yíyàng zhòngyào. Tā jīng rén jièshào zhǎodàole yígè hěn hépāi de yíngyǎng shī. Yíngyǎng shī ràng tā bǎ chī de suǒyǒu dōngxi dōu jìlù xiàlái. Jiē xiàlái de jǐ gè yuè, Àolì gǎibiànle yìxiē huài de yǐnshí xíguàn, zài tígāo dànbáizhì shè rù liàng de tóngshí, yě jiǎnshǎole tànshuǐ huàhéwù de shè rù liàng. Àolì yuè pǎo yuè kuài, yuè kuài yuè xiǎng pǎo. Zhè jiǔ gè yuè de xùnliàn hěn chénggōng. Zài pǎo mǎlāsōng de dāngtiān, tā búdàn qīngsōng de yuèguòle zhōngdiǎn xiàn, érqiě yòng de shíjiān yě bǐ èrshíbā suì de nà cì mǎlāsōng shǎole hěnduō.

Oli is forty years old; his favorite sports are playing football (soccer) and running marathons. He ran a marathon when he was twenty-eight. He was young and didn't train much, but the whole week after running the marathon, his whole body ached, and he couldn't walk for three days. This time he planned to prepare well, and he gave himself nine months. He joined a running club close to his home. He also knows that training is important, and nutrition and rest are just as important as training. He was introduced to a nutritionist that he gets along with. The nutritionist asked him to record everything he ate. Over the next

few months, Oli changed some of his bad eating habits, increasing his protein intake while reducing his carbohydrate intake. Oli ran faster and faster, and the faster he ran the more he wanted to run. The nine months of training were very successful. On the day of the marathon, he not only crossed the finish line with ease, but also took less time than the marathon he ran at the age of twenty-eight.

生词/Vocabulary List

- 平时 – píngshí: usually
- 参加 – cānjiā: to participate in, to take part in
- 得 – děi: have to
- 打橄榄球 – dǎ gǎnlǎnqiú: to play rugby
- 跑马拉松 – pǎo mǎlāsōng: run a marathon
- 训练 – xùnliàn: to train
- 马马虎虎 – mǎmǎhūhū: so-so, not taking something seriously
- 整个 – zhěnggè: entire
- 全身 – quánshēn: whole body
- 疼痛 – téngtòng: to ache, pain
- 尤其 – yóuqí: especially
- 吸取 – xīqǔ: to learn from, to absorb
- 俱乐部 – jùlèbù: club
- 会员 – huìyuán: member
- 信息 – xìnxī: information
- 伙伴 – huǒbàn: partner, buddy
- 营养 – yíngyǎng: nutrition
- 休息 – xiūxi: to rest, rest

- 同样 – tóngyàng: same
- 经 – jīng: through
- 介绍 – jièshào: to introduce
- 合拍 – hépāi: to get along with
- 营养师 – yíngyǎng shī: nutritionist
- 头 – tóu: head
- 记录 – jìlù: to keep a log, to record
- 麻烦 – máfan: hassle, trouble
- 浪费 – làngfèi: to waste, waste
- 老老实实 – lǎolǎo-shíshí: sincere, strictly
- 日记 – rìjì: journal
- 表明 – biǎomíng: to show, to indicate
- 碳水化合物 – tànshuǐ huàhéwù: carbohydrate
- 蛋白质 – dànbáizhì: protein
- 改变 – gǎibiàn: to change, change
- 坏 – huài: bad
- 习惯 – xíguàn: habit
- 提高 – tígāo: to improve

91

- 摄入量 – shè rù liàng: intake
- 减少 – jiǎnshǎo: to reduce, to decrease
- 无可挑剔 – wú kě tiāoti: impeccable
- 遵循 – zūnxún: to follow
- 百分之百– bǎifēnzhībǎi: hundred percent
- 良性循环 – liángxìng xúnhuán: virtuous circle
- 轻松 – qīngsōng: relaxed
- 越过 – yuè guò: go over
- 终点线 – zhōngdiǎn xiàn: finish line

问题/Questions

1. 奥利四十岁，可是他看起来很老。

   Oli is forty years old, but he looks old.

   A. 对
   B. 错

2. 奥利二十八岁的时候已经跑过一次马拉松了。

   Oli already ran a marathon once when he was twenty-eight years old.

   A. 对
   B. 错

3. 奥利和他的跑步伙伴是什么关系？

   What kind of relationship does Oli have with his running buddy?

   A. 朋友关系
   B. 同学关系
   C. 同事关系
   D. 邻居关系

4. 找到一个营养师后，奥利提高了什么的摄入量？

   After getting a nutritionist, what intake has Oli increased?

   A. 蛋白质
   B. 碳水化合物
   C. 水
   D. 蔬菜

5. 奥利四十岁跑马拉松用的时间比二十八岁那次用的少。

   Oli ran a marathon at age 40 in less time than he did at age 28.

   A. 对
   B. 错

答案/Answers

1. B 错
   False

2. A 对
   True

3. B 同学关系
   Classmate relation

4. A 蛋白质
   Protein

5. A 对
   True

CHAPTER 8

好漂亮的家！–
WHAT A BEAUTIFUL HOME!

我最近新**交**了一个朋友，他是我一个好朋友的朋友。

上个星期他邀请我到他家**做客**。没有想到的是：他家的**装修**极具特色。

他住的**楼房**一共有三层。他家是最**顶上**的一层。他们的楼没有**电梯**，我只好**以步代梯**了！

他家是两**室**一厅，带两个**洗手间**，一个阳台和一个**车库**。居住面积大概有 80 平方米。

一进门**就**看到棕色的**木地板**，走廊很**宽**很亮，让人觉得很舒服。离门一米左右，左边**靠**墙放着一个**法式**的浅棕色的木桌。木桌上**摆放**着两三个**相框**和一**盆**兰花。相片里是他在**非洲**的家人，有他的爸爸妈妈、姐姐、妹妹和弟弟。木桌的上方有一个**圆形**的镜子。镜子和相框都是**金属质地**的，很漂亮。再往前走，可以看到走廊两边的墙上挂着几**幅**非洲**现代**的艺术**作品**。这些艺术作品是非洲年青女性的**头像照**。她们来自于一些最有名的非洲**部落**。照片中她们**戴**着自己部落传统的**头饰**。这些艺术作品的**颜色很鲜艳**，作品有点儿**抽象派**的味道，可是再**仔细**看一看，它们又很**现实**，作品中的年轻女性都是**生活**中的真人。

两间**卧室**在走廊的左边。第一间是**主卧室**，带洗手间。主卧室是**长方形**的，面积有二十平方米左右。主卧室里面有一张**双人床**、两个**床头柜**、一个**大衣柜**和一张**皮沙发椅**。对着床的墙上有几张黑白的**自然**风景的**帆布画**。床、床头柜和大衣柜都是浅棕色的，和墙上的黑白帆布画一起看起来很自然，让人感觉很**接地气**。**次卧室**的面积**稍微**小一点，里面有一张很大的**办公桌**和一把**靠背椅**。这是他的**书房**。最近两年由于新冠肺炎的原因，他一直在家上班。主卧室和次卧室的一边都是很大的**窗户**，两个房间里整天都**阳光充足**。走廊的右边是一个洗手间，里面有**盆浴**、**淋浴**、**大理石**的**洗手盆**和**坐便器**。洗手盆的上方是一整面的**化妆镜**。化妆镜是挂在后面一整墙的柜子前面的，又**美观**又**实用**。

走廊的**另一端**是客厅和厨房。现在的客厅都是**开放式**的，他家也不**例外**。他家客厅的装饰真是一**绝**。客厅四面的墙都是**墨绿色**的，绿色**属于冷色调**，墨绿色**营造**了一种**宁静悠远**的感觉，让人**放松**，并且感到**精神振作**。客厅里的**沙发**是**芥末黄**，沙发后面的墙上有一幅黑色的**油画**，在油画的中间**探出**了一个老虎头，**猛地一**看你会**吓一跳**，吓一跳的同时你又会**觉察**到这只老虎**其实很顺服**。对着油画的墙上挂着一个**巨屏超薄**的电视。沙发的右边连着一个小阳台，坐在阳台上面对的是楼前面**静静**的河。客厅里的**家具**很少，只有一个小**装饰柜**和一个**酒柜**。厨房里**现代化**的家庭厨具一应俱全。zhe

好漂亮的家！– What a Beautiful Home!
With English Translation

我最近新**交**了一个朋友，他是我一个好朋友的朋友。

Wǒ zuìjìn xīn **jiāo**le yígè péngyǒu, tā shì wǒ yígè hǎo péngyǒu de péngyǒu.

I recently **made** a new friend who is a friend of a good friend of mine.

上个星期他邀请我到他家**做客**。没有想到的是：他家的**装修**极具特色。

Shàng gè xīngqī tā yāoqǐng wǒ dào tā jiā **zuòkè**. Méiyǒu xiǎngdào de shì: Tā jiā de **zhuāngxiū** jí **jù** tèsè.

He invited me to his house last week. What I didn't expect was: the **decoration** of his home **shows** distinguishing charac teristics.

他住的**楼房**一共有三层。他家是最**顶上**的一层。他们的楼没有**电梯**，我只好**以步代梯**了！

Tā zhù de **lóufáng** yígòng yǒu sān **céng**. Tā jiā shì zuì **dǐng shàng** de yì céng. Tāmen de lóu méiyǒu **diàntī**, wǒ zhǐhǎo **yǐ bù dài tī**le!

The **storied building** where he lives has three **floors**. His house is **on the top floor**. There is no **elevator** in the building, so I had to **use the stairs instead**!

他家是两**室**一**厅**，带两个**洗手间**、一个**阳台**和一个**车库**。居住面积大概有 80 平方米。

Tā jiā shì liǎng **shì** yì **tīng**, **dài** liǎng gè **xǐshǒujiān**, yígè **yángtái** hé yígè **chēkù**. **Jūzhù** miànjī dàgài yǒu 80 píngfāng mǐ.

His home has two **bedrooms** and one **living room**, with two **bathrooms**, a **balcony** and a **garage**. The **living** area is about 80 square meters.

一进门**就**看到棕色的**木地板**，**走廊**很**宽**很**亮**，让人觉得很舒服。离门一米左右，左边**靠**墙放着一个**法式**的浅棕色的木桌。

Yí jìnmén **jiù** kàn dào zōngsè de **mù dìbǎn**, **zǒuláng** hěn **kuān** hěn **liàng**, ràng rén juéde hěn shūfu. Lí mén yì mǐ zuǒyòu, zuǒbiān **kào** qiáng fàngzhe yígè **fǎshì** de **qiǎn** zōngsè de mù zhuō.

As soon as you enter the door, you see the brown **wooden floor**, and the **hallway** is **wide** and **bright**, making people feel very comfortable. About one meter away from the door, on the left **against** the wall there is a **French-style light** brown wooden table.

木桌上**摆放**着两三个**相框**和一**盆兰花**。**相片**里是他在**非洲**的家人，有他的爸爸妈妈，姐姐，妹妹和弟弟。

Mù zhuō shàng **bǎi fàng** zhe liǎng sān gè **xiàngkuàng** hé yì**pén lánhuā**. **Xiàngpiàn** lǐ shì tā zài **Fēizhōu** de jiārén, yǒu tā de bàba māma, jiějie, mèimei hé dìdi.

There are two or three picture **frames** and a **pot** of **orchids** on the wooden table. In the **photos**, you can see his family in **Africa**, including his parents, elder sister, younger sister and younger brother.

木桌的上方有一个**圆形**的镜子。镜子和相框都是**金属质地**的，很漂亮。再往前走，可以看到走廊两边的墙上**挂**着几**幅**非洲**现代**的艺术**作品**。

Mù zhuō de shàngfāng yǒu yígè **yuán xíng** de jìngzi. Jìngzi hé xiàngkuāng dōu shì **jīnshǔ zhìdì** de, hěn piàoliang. Zài wǎng qián zǒu, kěyǐ kàn dào zǒuláng liǎngbiān de qiáng shàng **guà**zhe jǐ **fú** Fēizhōu **xiàndài** de yìshù **zuòpǐn**.

There is a **round** mirror above the wooden table. The mirrors and picture frames are all **metal** and are beautiful. Further up the hallway, you can see several African **modern artworks hanging** on the walls on both sides.

这些艺术作品是非洲年青女性的**头像照**。她们来自于一些最有名的非洲**部落**。照片中她们**戴**着自己部落传统的头饰。

Zhèxiē yìshù zuòpǐn shì Fēizhōu niánqīng nǚxìng de **tóuxiàng zhào**. Tāmen láizì yú yìxiē zuì yǒumíng de Fēizhōu **bùluò**. Zhàopiàn zhōng tāmen **dài**zhe zìjǐ bùluò chuántǒng de **tóushì**.

The artworks are **portraits** of young African women. They come from some of the most famous African **tribes**. They are pictured **wearing** their own tribal traditional **headdress**.

这些艺术作品的**颜色**很**鲜艳**，作品有点儿**抽象派**的味道，可是再**仔细**看一看，它们又很**现实**，作品中的年轻女性都是**生活**中的真人。

Zhèxiē yìshù zuòpǐn de **yánsè** hěn **xiānyàn**, zuòpǐn yǒudiǎnr **chōuxiàng pài** de wèidào, kěshì zài **zǐxì** kàn yi kàn, tāmen yòu hěn **xiànshí**, zuòpǐn zhōng de niánqīng nǚxìng dōu shì **shēnghuó** zhōng de zhēnrén.

The **colors** of these artworks are very **bright**, and the artworks are a bit **abstract**, but if you look **closely**, they are very **realistic**. The young women in the artworks are people in real **life**.

两间**卧室**在走廊的左边。第一间是**主卧室**，带洗手间。主卧室是**长方形**的，面积有二十平方米左右。主卧室里面有一张**双人床**、两个**床头柜**、一个**大衣柜**和一张**皮沙发椅**。

Liǎng jiān **wòshì** zài zǒuláng de zuǒbiān. Dì yī jiàn shì **zhǔ wòshì**, dài xǐshǒujiān. Zhǔ wòshì shì **chángfāngxíng** de, miànjī yǒu èrshí píngfāng mǐ zuǒyòu. Zhǔ wòshì lǐmiàn yǒu yìzhāng **shuāngrén chuáng**, liǎnggè **chuángtóuguì**, yígè **dà yīguì** hé yìzhāng **pí shāfā yǐ**.

The two **bedrooms** are on the left side of the hallway. The first is the **master bedroom** with bathroom. The master bedroom is **rectangular** with an area of about twenty square meters. The master bedroom has a **double bed**, two **bedside tables**, a large **wardrobe** and a **leather sofa chair**.

对着床的墙上有几张黑白的**自然**风景的**帆布画**。床、床头柜和大衣柜都是浅棕色的，和墙上的黑白布画一起看起来很自然，让人感觉很**接地气**。

Duìzhe chuáng de qiáng shàng yǒu jǐ zhāng hēibái de **zìrán** fēngjǐng de **fānbù huà**. Chuáng, chuángtóuguì hé dà yīguì dōu shì qiǎn zōngsè de, hé qiáng shàng de hēibái bù huà yìqǐ kàn qǐlái hěn zìrán, ràng rén gǎnjué hěn **jiē dì qì**.

Facing the bed, there are several black and white **canvases** of **natural** scenery on the wall. The bed, bedside table and large wardrobe are all light brown, which together with the black and white canvas on the wall look natural and make you feel **grounded**.

次卧室的面积**稍微**小一点，里面有一张很大的**办公桌**和一把**靠背椅**。这是他的**书房**。最近两年由于新冠肺炎的原因，他一直在家上班。

Cì wòshì de miànjī **shāowéi** xiǎo yìdiǎn, lǐmiàn yǒu yìzhāng hěn dà de **bàngōng zhuō** hé yìbǎ **kàobèi yǐ**. Zhè shì tā de **shūfáng**. Zuìjìn liǎng nián yóuyú xīnguān fèiyán de yuányīn, tā yìzhí zài jiā shàngbān.

The **second bedroom** is **slightly** smaller, with a large **desk** and a **high-back chair**. This is his **study**. He has been working from home for the past two years due to COVID-19.

主卧室和次卧室的一边都是很大的**窗户**，两个房间里整天都**阳光**充足。

Zhǔ wòshì hé cì wòshì de yìbiān dōu shì hěn dà de **chuānghu**, liǎng gè fángjiān lǐ zhěng tiān dōu **yángguāng** chōngzú.

Both the master and second bedrooms have large **windows** on one side; both rooms get plenty of **sunlight** all day.

走廊的右边是一个洗手间，里面有**盆浴**、**淋浴**、**大理石**的**洗手盆**和**坐便器**。洗手盆的上方是一整面的**化妆镜**。化妆镜是挂在后面一整墙的柜子前面的，又**美观**又**实用**。

Zǒuláng de yòubiān shì yígè xǐshǒujiān, lǐmiàn yǒu **pényù**, **línyù**, **dàlǐshí** de **xǐshǒu pén** hé **zuò biàn qì**. Xǐshǒu pén de shàngfāng shì yì zhěng miàn de **huàzhuāng jìng**. Huàzhuāng jìng shì guà zài hòumiàn yì zhěng qiáng de guìzi qiánmiàn de, yòu **měiguān** yòu **shíyòng**.

On the right side of the hallway is a bathroom with a **tub**, **shower**, **marble wash basin** and **toilet**. Above the wash basin is a full-size **vanity mirror**. The vanity mirror is hung in front of the cabinet with a whole wall at the back, which is both **good to look at** and **practical**.

走廊的**另一端**是客厅和厨房。现在的客厅都是**开放式**的，他家也不**例外**。他家客厅的装饰真是一**绝**。

Zǒuláng de **lìng yìduān** shì kètīng hé chúfáng. Xiànzài de kètīng dōu shì **kāifàng shì** de, tā jiā yě bú **lìwài**. Tā jiā kètīng de zhuāngshì zhēn shì **yì jué**.

At **the other end of** the hallway is the living room and kitchen. Now, living rooms are made in **open style**, and his house is no **exception**. The decor of his living room is truly **amazing**.

客厅四面的墙都是**墨绿色**的，绿色**属于冷色调**，墨绿色**营造**了一种**宁静悠远**的感觉，让人**放松**，并且感到**精神振作**。

Kètīng sìmiàn de qiáng dōu shì **mò lǜsè** de, lǜsè **shǔyú lěng sèdiào**, mò lǜsè **yíngzàole** yìzhǒng **níngjìng yōuyuǎn** de gǎnjué, ràng rén **fàngsōng**, bìngqiě gǎndào **jīngshén zhènzuò**.

The walls on all four sides of the living room are **dark green**, green is a **cool color**, and the dark green **creates** a sense of **tranquility** and **distance** from everyday life which makes people **relax** and feel **refreshed**.

客厅里的**沙发**是**芥末黄**，沙发后面的墙上有一幅黑色的**油画**，在油画的中间**探出**了一个老虎头，**猛地**一看你会**吓一跳**，吓一跳的同时你又会**觉察**到这只老虎**其实**很**顺服**。

Kètīng lǐ de **shāfā** shì **jièmò huáng**, shāfā hòumiàn de qiáng shàng yǒu yìfú hēisè de **yóuhuà**, zài yóuhuà de zhōngjiān **tàn chū**le yígè lǎohǔ tóu, **měng de** yí kàn nǐ huì **xià yí tiào**, xià yí tiào de tóngshí nǐ yòu huì **juéchá** dào zhè zhǐ lǎohǔ **qíshí** hěn **shùnfú**.

The **sofa** in the living room is **mustard color**, and the wall behind the sofa is a black **oil painting**. In the middle of the oil painting, a tiger's head **pops up**. If you look at it **suddenly**, you will be **startled**. At the same time, you will also **notice** that the tiger was **actually tame**.

对着油画的墙上挂着一个**巨屏超薄**的电视。沙发的右边连着一个小阳台，坐在阳台上面对的是楼前面**静静**的河。

Duìzhe yóuhuà de qiáng shàng guàzhe yígè **jù píng chāo báo** de diànshì. Shāfā de yòubiān liánzhe yígè xiǎo yángtái, zuò zài yángtái shàng miàn duì de shì lóu qiánmiàn **jìng jìng** de hé.

A **huge, ultra-thin** TV hangs on the wall facing the oil painting. To the right of the sofa there is a small balcony and sitting on the balcony, you would face the **quiet** river in front of the building.

客厅里的**家具**很少，只有一个小**装饰柜**和一个**酒柜**。厨房里**现代**化的家庭厨具一应俱全。

Kètīng lǐ de **jiājù** hěn shǎo, zhǐyǒu yígè xiǎo **zhuāngshì guì** hé yígè **jiǔ guì**. Chúfáng lǐ **xiàndàihuà** de **jiātíng chújù yìyīng-jùquán**.

There is very little **furniture** in the living room, only a small **decorative cabinet** and a **wine cabinet**. The kitchen is fully **stocked with modern household kitchen appliances**.

总结/Summary

我新交的一个朋友请我到他家做客。他家两室一厅，带两个洗手间、一个阳台和一个车库，居住面积大概有 80 平方米。棕色的木地板让人觉得很舒服。走廊墙上的两边挂着几幅非洲现代的艺术作品。这些作品的颜色很鲜艳，有抽象派的味道，但是这些作品里的年轻女孩都是生活中的真人。两间卧室都在走廊的左边，房间内阳光充足。走廊的右边是洗手间。走廊的另一端是客厅和厨房。客厅四面的墙都是墨绿色的。沙发是芥末黄。沙发后面的墙上挂着一张油画。客厅里的家具很少。厨房里现代的家庭厨具一应俱全。

Wǒ xīn jiāo de yígè péngyǒu qǐng wǒ dào tā jiā zuòkè. Tā jiā liǎng shì yì tīng, dài liǎng gè xǐshǒujiān, yígè yángtái hé yígè chēkù, jūzhù miànjī dàgài yǒu 80 píngfāng mǐ. Zōngsè de mù dìbǎn ràng rén juéde hěn shūfu. Zǒuláng qiáng shàng de liǎngbiān guàzhe jǐ fú Fēizhōu xiàndài de yìshù zuòpǐn. Zhèxiē zuòpǐn de yánsè hěn xiānyàn, yǒu chōuxiàng pài de wèidào, dànshì zhèxiē zuòpǐn lǐ de niánqīng nǚhái dōu shì shēnghuó zhōng de zhēnrén. Liǎng jiān wòshì dōu zài zǒuláng de zuǒbiān, fángjiān nèi yángguāng chōngzú. Zǒuláng de yòubiān shì xǐshǒujiān. Zǒuláng de lìng yìduān shì kètīng hé chúfáng. Kètīng sìmiàn de qiáng dōu shì mò lǜsè de. Shāfā shì jièmò huáng. Shāfā hòumiàn de qiáng shàng guàzhe yìzhāng yóuhuà. Kètīng lǐ de jiājù hěn shǎo. Chúfáng lǐ xiàndài de jiātíng chújù yìyīng-jùquán.

A new friend I made invited me to his house as a guest. His house has two bedrooms and one living room, with two bathrooms, a balcony and a garage. The living area is about 80 square meters. The brown wooden floor makes people feel very comfortable. There are several pieces of African modern art hanging on both sides of the hallway. The colors of these artworks are bright and abstract, but the young women in these artworks are people in real life. Both bedrooms are on the left side of the hallway, and the rooms are full of sunlight. To the right of the hallway is the bathroom. At the other end of the hallway are the living room and kitchen. The walls on all four sides of the living room are dark green. The sofa is mustard yellow. An oil painting hangs on the wall behind the sofa. There is very little furniture in the living room. The kitchen is fully stocked with modern household kitchen appliances.

生词/Vocabulary List

- 交 – jiāo: to make friends
- 做客 – zuòkè: to be a guest
- 装修 – zhuāngxiū: to furnish
- 具 – jù: to have
- 楼房 – lóufáng: storied building
- 层 – céng: floor
- 顶上 – dǐng shàng: on the top
- 电梯 – diàntī: lift
- 以步代梯 – yǐ bù dài tī: walk instead taking the lift
- 室 – shì: room, bedroom
- 厅 – tīng: hall, living room
- 带 – dài: to come with
- 洗手间 – xǐshǒujiān: bathroom
- 阳台 – yángtái: balcony
- 车库 – chēkù: garage
- 居住 – jūzhù: to live, living
- 一…就 – yī…jiù: as soon as…
- 木地板 – mù dìbǎn: wooden floor
- 走廊 – zǒuláng: hallway
- 宽 – kuān: wide
- 亮 – liàng: bright
- 法式 – fǎshì: French style
- 浅 – qiǎn: light, shallow
- 摆放 – bǎi fàng: to place, to put
- 相框 – xiàngkuāng: photo frame
- 盆 – pén: pot, measure word for plants placed inside pots
- 兰花 – lánhuā: orchid
- 相片 – xiàngpiàn: photo
- 圆形 – yuán xíng: round
- 金属 – jīnshǔ: metal
- 质地 – zhìdì: texture
- 挂 – guà: to hang
- 幅 – fú: measure word for paintings
- 现代 – xiàndài: modern
- 作品 – zuòpǐn: work
- 头像照 – tóuxiàng zhào: portrait
- 部落 – bùluò: tribe
- 戴 – dài: to wear
- 头饰 – tóushì: headdress
- 颜色 – yánsè: color
- 鲜艳 – xiānyàn: bright
- 抽象派 – chōuxiàng pài: abstractionism
- 仔细 – zǐxì: carefulness

- 现实 – xiànshí: reality
- 生活 – shēnghuó: life
- 卧室 – wòshì: bedroom
- 主卧室 – zhǔ wòshì: master bedroom
- 长方形 – chángfāngxíng: rectangle
- 双人床 – shuāngrén chuáng: double bed
- 床头柜 – chuángtóuguì: bedside table
- 大衣柜 – dà yīguì: big closet
- 皮 – pí: leather
- 沙发椅 – shāfā yǐ: sofa chair
- 自然 – zìrán: nature
- 帆布画 – fānbù huà: canvas
- 接地气 – jiē dì qì: grounded
- 次卧室 – cì wòshì: second bedroom
- 稍微 – shāowéi: slightly, a little bit
- 办公桌 – bàngōng zhuō: office desk
- 靠背椅 – kàobèi yǐ: high back chair
- 书房 – shūfáng: study room
- 窗户 – chuānghu: window
- 阳光 – yángguāng: sunlight
- 盆浴 – pényù: bathtub
- 淋浴 – línyù: shower, to take a shower
- 大理石 – dàlǐshí: marble
- 洗手盆 – xǐshǒu pén: wash basin, sink
- 坐便器 – zuò biàn qì: toilet
- 化妆镜 – huàzhuāng jìng: vanity mirror
- 美观 – měiguān: beautiful
- 实用 – shíyòng: practical
- 另 – lìng: other
- 一端 – yìduān: one end
- 开放式 – kāifàng shì: open style
- 例外 – lìwài: exception
- 一绝 – yì jué: amazing
- 墨绿色 – mò lǜsè: dark green
- 属于 – shǔyú: to be classified
- 冷色调 – lěng sèdiào: cool colors
- 营造 – yíngzào: to create, to build
- 宁静 – níngjìng: peaceful, tranquil
- 悠远 – yōuyuǎn: distant, far away
- 放松 – fàngsōng: to relax

- 精神振作 – jīngshén zhènzuò: refreshed
- 芥末黄 – jièmò huáng: mustard yellow
- 油画 – yóuhuà: oil painting
- 探出 – tàn chū: to pop up
- 猛地 – měng de: abruptly
- 吓一跳 – xià yí tiào: to be startled
- 觉察 – juéchá: to be aware
- 其实 – qíshí: actually, in fact
- 顺服 – shùnfú: submissive, to obey
- 巨屏 – jù píng: giant screen
- 超薄 – chāo báo: ultra-thin
- 静静 – jìng jìng: quiet
- 家具 – jiājù: furniture
- 装饰柜 – zhuāngshì guì: decorative cabinet
- 酒柜 – jiǔ guì: wine cabinet
- 现代化 – xiàndàihuà: modernization, to modernize
- 家庭 – jiātíng: household
- 厨具 – chújù: kitchen appliances
- 一应俱全 – yìyīng-jùquán: everything is available

问题/Questions

1. 我新交的朋友住的楼房没有电梯。

   My new friend lives in a building without an elevator。

   A. 对
   B. 错

2. 我新交的朋友家里没有阳台。

   My new friend doesn't have a balcony at home.

   A. 对
   B. 错

3. 非洲年轻女孩的头像照挂在哪里？

   Where are the artworks of young African women hanging?

   A. 走廊的墙上。
   B. 主卧室的墙上。
   C. 客厅的墙上。
   D. 厨房的墙上。

4. 客厅和卧室的家具都很多。

   There is a lot of furniture in both the living room and bedrooms.

   A. 对
   B. 错

5. 厨房里现代家庭厨具一应俱全。

   The kitchen is fully stocked with modern kitchen appliances.

   A. 对
   B. 错

答案/Answers

1. A 对
   True

2. B 错
   False

3. A 走廊的墙上
   On the walls of the hallway.

4. B 错
   False

5. A 对
   True

CHAPTER 9

维多利亚的新星期五 –
VICTORIA'S NEW FRIDAYS

维多利亚是一位护士，在医院工作。从今年八月起，维多利亚不上全职了，现在每个星期她只上四天班，星期五到星期日休息。

星期五做什么好呢？维多利亚的女儿建议妈妈做一些有意思的事情，比如说：学普通话，下饭馆儿，参观伦敦的各大博物馆等等。维多利亚觉得女儿的建议好极了！

为什么要学习普通话呢？维多利亚虽然住在英国伦敦，但是她其实是马来西亚华人。她的祖籍是中国广东，她是在马来西亚出生和长大的。在马来西亚她上的是英文学校，所以从来没学过普通话。近些年来，随着中国经济的发展和世界地位的提高，普通话越来越流行，维多利亚就有了学习普通话的愿望。她希望有一天能回到中国广东看看，所以会说一些普通话是很有必要的。上个星期她在谷歌商家网页上看了看，联系了一个离她家不太远的普通话家教。她们当天晚上就打了一个视频电话，谈了谈有关细节，一切都谈定了，下个星期五开始上一对一的中文网课。

维多利亚很爱吃广东菜。到了英国伦敦以后，维多利亚一家只有在特别场合才会到广东饭馆儿吃地道的中国菜。维多利亚的最爱是广东早茶。她打算八月的每个星期五都去伦敦市中心中国城的广东饭馆儿喝地道的广东早茶。

维多利亚也是一个博物馆**迷**。从小的时候，她就很喜欢**历史**和**美术**课。记得她刚来伦敦的头两年，她每几个星期都会去博物馆。伦敦有那么**多世界一流**的博物馆。她了解到了更多的世界文化、历史和艺术。过了几年，她结了婚，女儿出生了，她成了妈妈，再也没有时间去博物馆了。现在好了，星期五不上班了，她又可以像以前一样到伦敦各大博物馆看看。从哪一个开始呢？**英国大英博物馆、维多利亚和阿尔伯特博物馆**,、**自然历史博物馆、国家画廊、伦敦博物馆**... 选择太多了！

维多利亚的新星期五– Victoria's New Fridays
With English Translation

维多利亚是一位护士，在医院工作。从今年八月起，维多利亚不上全职了，现在每个星期她只上四天班，星期五到星期日休息。

Wéiduōlìyà shì **yíwèi hùshì**, zài yīyuàn gōngzuò. Cóng jīnnián bā yuè qǐ, Wéiduōlìyà bú shàng **quánzhí**le, xiànzài měi gè xīngqī tā zhǐ shàng sì tiān bān, xīngqīwǔ dào xīngqīrì xiūxi.

Victoria is **a nurse** and works in a hospital. Since August this year, Victoria has stopped working **full-time**, and now she only works four days a week, off from Friday to Sunday.

星期五做什么好呢？维多利亚的女儿建议妈妈做一些有意思的事情，比如说：学普通话，下饭馆儿，参观伦敦的各大博物馆等等。维多利亚觉得女儿的建议好极了！

Xīngqīwǔ zuò shénme hǎo ne? Wéiduōlìyà de nǚ'ér jiànyì māma zuò yìxiē yǒu yìsi de shìqing, bǐrú shuō: Xué **Pǔtōnghuà**, xià fànguǎnr, **cānguān** Lúndūn de gè dà **bówùguǎn** děng děng. Wéiduōlìyà juéde nǚ'ér de jiànyì hǎo jí le!

What does she do on Fridays? Victoria's daughter suggested that her mother do something interesting, such as: learning **Mandarin**, going to restaurants, **visiting** major **museums** in London. Victoria thought her daughter's suggestion was great!

为什么要学习普通话呢？维多利亚虽然住在英国伦敦，但是她其实是马来西亚华人。她的祖籍是中国广东，她是在马来西亚出生和长大的。

Wèishénme yào xuéxí Pǔtōnghuà ne? Wéiduōlìyà suīrán zhù zài Yīngguó Lúndūn, dànshì tā qíshí shì **Mǎláixīyà huárén**. Tā de **zǔjí** shì Zhōngguó **Guǎngdōng**, tā shì zài Mǎláixīyà chūshēng hé zhǎng dà de.

113

Why learn Mandarin? Although Victoria lives in London, England, she is in fact **Malaysian Chinese**. Her **ancestral home** is **Guangdong**, China, and she was born and raised in Malaysia.

在马来西亚她上的是英文学校，所以从来没学过普通话。**近些年来，随着**中国**经济**的发展和世界**地位**的提高，普通话越来越流行，维多利亚就有了学习普通话的**愿望**。

Zài Mǎláixīyà tā shàng de shì Yīngwén xuéxiào, suǒyǐ cónglái méi xuéguò Pǔtōnghuà. **Jìn xiē niánlái, suízhe** Zhōngguó **jīngjì** de fǎzhǎn hé shìjiè **dìwèi** de tígāo, Pǔtōnghuà yuè lái yuè liúxíng, Wéiduōlìyà jiù yǒule xuéxí Pǔtōnghuà de **yuànwàng**.

In Malaysia, she went to an English school, so she never learned Mandarin. **In recent years**, **with** the development of China's **economy** and the improvement of its **status** in the world, Mandarin has become more and more popular, and Victoria has the **desire** to learn Mandarin.

她希望有一天能回到中国广东看看，所以会说一些普通话是很有**必要**的。上个星期她在**谷歌商家网页**上看了看，联系了一个离她家不太远的普通话**家教**。

Tā xīwàng yǒu yìtiān néng huí dào Zhōngguó Guǎngdōng kàn kan, suǒyǐ huì shuō yìxiē Pǔtōnghuà shì hěn yǒu **bìyào** de. Shàng gè xīngqī tā zài **Gǔgē shāngjiā wǎngyè** shàng kàn le kàn, liánxìle yígè lí tā jiā bú tài yuǎn de Pǔtōnghuà **jiājiào**.

She hopes to visit Guangdong, China one day, so it is **necessary** to speak some Mandarin. Last week she looked at the **Google Business page** and contacted a Mandarin **tutor** not too far from her home.

她们当天晚上就打了一个**视频**电话，谈了谈**有关细节**，一切都谈定了，下个星期五开始上一对一的中文网课。

Tāmen dāngtiān wǎnshang jiù dǎle yígè **shìpín** diànhuà, **tán**le tán **yǒuguān xìjié**, yíqiè dōu **tán dìng**le, xià gè xīngqīwǔ kāishǐ shàng **yī duì yī** de Zhōngwén wǎng kè.

They made a **video** call that night and **talked about** the **related details**. Everything was **negotiated**. Next Friday, they will have **one-on-one** Chinese online classes.

维多利亚很爱吃广东菜。到了英国伦敦以后，维多利亚一家只有在**特别场合**才会到广东饭馆儿吃地道的中国菜。

Wéiduōlìyà hěn ài chī Guǎngdōng cài. Dàole Yīngguó Lúndūn yǐhòu, Wéiduōlìyà yìjiā zhǐyǒu zài **tèbié chǎnghé** cái huì dào Guǎngdōng fànguǎnr chī dìdào de Zhōngguó cài.

Victoria loves Cantonese food. After arriving in London, England, her family only went to Cantonese restaurants to eat authentic Chinese food **on special occasions**.

维多利亚的最爱是广东早茶。她打算八月的每个星期五都去伦敦市中心**中国城**的广东饭馆儿喝地道的广东早茶。

Wéiduōlìyà de zuì ài shì Guǎngdōng zǎochá. Tā dǎsuàn bā yuè de měi gè xīngqīwǔ dōu qù Lúndūn shì zhōngxīn **Zhōngguó chéng** de Guǎngdōng fànguǎnr hē dìdào de Guǎngdōng zǎochá.

Victoria's favorite is Cantonese morning tea. She plans to go to the Cantonese restaurant in Central London's **Chinatown** every Friday in August for authentic Cantonese morning tea.

维多利亚也是一个博物馆**迷**。从小的时候，她就很喜欢**历史**和**美术**课。记得她刚来伦敦的头两年，她每几个星期都会去博物馆。伦敦有那么多**世界一流**的博物馆。她了解到了更多的世界文化、历史和艺术。

Wéiduōlìyà yě shì yígè bówùguǎn **mí**. Cóngxiǎo de shíhou, tā jiù hěn xǐhuān **lìshǐ** hé **měishù** kè. Jìdé tā gāng lái Lúndūn de tóu liǎng nián, tā měi jǐ gè xīngqī dōu huì qù bówùguǎn. Lúndūn yǒu nàme duō **shìjiè yīliú** de bówùguǎn. Tā liǎojiě dàole gèng duō de shìjiè wénhuà, lìshǐ hé yìshù.

Victoria is also a museum **fan**. From an early age, she enjoyed **history** and **art** classes. During her first two years in London, Victoria went to some museums every few weeks. There are so many **world-class** museums in London. She learned more about world culture, history and art.

过了几年，她结了婚，女儿出生了，她成了妈妈，再也没有时间去博物馆了。现在好了，星期五不上班了，她又可以像以前一样到伦敦各大博物馆看看。

Guòle jǐ nián, tā jiéle hūn, nǚ'ér chūshēngle, tā chéngle māma, zài yě méiyǒu shíjiān qù bówùguǎn le. Xiànzài hǎole, xīngqīwǔ bú shàngbānle, tā yòu kěyǐ xiàng yǐqián yíyàng dào Lúndūn gè dà bówùguǎn kàn kan.

After a few years, she got married, her daughter was born, she became a mother, and she no longer had time to go to the museum. Well, now that she doesn't go to work on Fridays anymore, she can go to the various big museums in London as before.

从哪一个开始呢？英国大英博物馆、维多利亚和阿尔伯特博物馆、自然历史博物馆、国家画廊、伦敦博物馆... 选择太多了!

Cóng nǎ yígè kāishǐ ne? **Yīngguó Dàyīng Bówùguǎn, Wéiduōlìyà hé Ā'ěrbótè Bówùguǎn, Zìrán Lìshǐ Bówùguǎn, Guójiā Huàláng,** Lúndūn Bówùguǎn... xuǎnzé tài duōle!

Which one to start with? **British Museum, Victoria and Albert Museum, Natural History Museum, National Gallery,** Museum of London... so many choices!

总结/Summary

维多利亚从今年八月起，每个星期只上四天班，星期五休息。女儿建议她学普通话，下饭馆儿，参观伦敦各大博物馆。维多利亚在谷歌商家网页上找到了一个普通话家教，打了一个视频电话后，从下个星期五开始上一对一的网课。维多利亚住在英国伦敦，可是她是在马来西亚出生的华人。她希望以后可以到广东看看。她也很喜欢吃广东早茶。八月的每个星期五她都要到伦敦市中心的中国城喝广东早茶。刚来伦敦的头两年，她每几个星期都到博物馆看看。她从小的时候就喜欢历史和美术，到伦敦以后，她了解到了更多的世界文化、历史和艺术。女儿出生以后，她就没有时间去博物馆了。现在好了，她又可以像以前一样常常去博物馆看看了。

Wéiduōlìyà cóng jīnnián bā yuè qǐ, měi gè xīngqī zhǐ shàng sì tiān bān, xīngqīwǔ xiūxi. Nǚ'ér jiànyì tā xué Pǔtōnghuà, xià fànguǎnr, cānjiā Lúndūn gè dà bówùguǎn. Wéiduōlìyà zài Gǔgē shāngjiā wǎngyè shàng zhǎodàole yígè Pǔtōnghuà jiājiào, dǎle yígè shìpín diànhuà hòu, cóng xià gè xīngqīwǔ kāishǐ shàng yī duì yī de wǎng kè. Wéiduōlìyà zhù zài Yīngguó Lúndūn, kěshì tā shì zài Mǎláixīyà chūshēng de huárén. Tā xīwàng yǐhòu kěyǐ dào Guǎngdōng kàn kan. Tā yě hěn xǐhuān chī Guǎngdōng zǎochá. Bā yuè de měi gè xīngqīwǔ tā dōu yào dào Lúndūn shì zhōngxīn de Zhōngguó chéng hē Guǎngdōng zǎochá. Gāng lái Lúndūn de tóu liǎng nián, tā měi jǐ gè xīngqī dōu dào bówùguǎn kàn kan. Tā cóngxiǎo de shíhou jiù xǐhuān lìshǐ hé měishù, dào Lúndūn yǐhòu, tā liǎojiě dàole gèng duō de shìjiè wénhuà, lìshǐ hé yìshù. Nǚ'ér chūshēng yǐhòu, tā jiù méiyǒu shíjiān qù bówùguǎnle. Xiànzài hǎole, tā yòu kěyǐ xiàng yǐqián yíyàng chángcháng qù bówùguǎn kàn kanle.

Since August this year, Victoria has only been working four days a week, with Fridays off. Her daughter suggested that she learn Mandarin, go to restaurants, and visit major museums in London. Victoria found a Mandarin tutor on the Google Business page, made a video call, and started one-on-one online lessons the next Friday. Victoria lives in London, England, but she is ethnically Chinese, born in Malaysia. She hopes to visit Guangdong in the future. She also likes to eat Yum Cha. Every Friday in August she goes to Chinatown in central London for Cantonese morning tea. For the first two years in London, she visited the museums every few weeks. She has been fond of history and fine arts since she was a child, and when she came to London, she learned more about world culture, history and art. After her daughter was born, she had no time to go to the museums. Well now, she can go to the museum as often as before.

生词/Vocabulary List

- 位 – wèi: a polite measure word used with people to show respect
- 护士 – hùshì: nurse
- 全职 – quánzhí: full time
- 普通话 – Pǔtōnghuà: Mandarin
- 参观 – cānguān: to visit
- 博物馆 – bówùguǎn: museum
- 马来西亚华人 – Mǎláixīyà huárén: Malaysian Chinese
- 祖籍 – zǔjí: ancestral home
- 广东 – Guǎngdōng: Guangdong
- 近些年来 – jìn xiē nián lái: in recent years
- 随着 – suízhe: along with
- 经济 – jīngjì: economy
- 地位 – dìwèi: status
- 愿望 – yuànwàng: desire
- 必要 – bìyào: necessary
- 谷歌 – Gǔgē: Google
- 商家 – shāngjiā: business
- 网页 – wǎngyè: web page
- 家教 – jiājiào: tutor
- 视频 – shìpín: video
- 谈 – tán: to talk about
- 有关 – yǒuguān: related
- 细节 – xìjié: details
- 谈定 – tán dìng: negotiated
- 一对一 – yī duì yī: one-to-one
- 特别场合 – tèbié chǎnghé: special occasion
- 中国城 – Zhōngguó chéng: China Town
- 迷 – mí: fan
- 历史 – lìshǐ: history
- 美术 – měishù: art
- 世界一流 – shìjiè yīliú: world class
- 英国大英博物馆 – Yīngguó Dàyīng Bówùguǎn: British Museum
- 维多利亚和阿尔伯特博物馆 – Wéiduōlìyà hé Ā'ěrbótè Bówùguǎn: Victoria & Albert Museum
- 自然历史博物馆 – Zìrán Lìshǐ Bówùguǎn: Natural History Museum
- 国家画廊 – Guójiā Huàláng: National Gallery

问题/Questions

1. 维多利亚星期一到星期五都上班。

   Victoria works Monday to Friday.

   A. 对
   B. 错

2. 维多利亚不喜欢喝广东早茶。

   Victoria does not like Cantonese morning tea.

   A. 对
   B. 错

3. 下面哪一个不是博物馆？

   Which of the following is not a museum?

   A. 大英博物馆
   B. 大英图书馆
   C. 维多利亚和阿尔伯特博物馆
   D. 自然历史博物馆

4. 维多利亚八月要去哪里的中国饭馆喝早茶？

   Whereabouts is the Chinese restaurant where Victoria is going to have Yum Cha in August?

   A. 伦敦市中心中国城
   B. 她家附近
   C. 医院旁边
   D. 她朋友家附近

5. 维多利亚想学哪种语言？

   Which language does Victoria want to learn?

   A. 英语
   B. 日语
   C. 普通话
   D. 韩语

答案/Answers

1. B 错
   False

2. B 错
   False

3. B 大英图书馆
   British Library

4. A 伦敦市中心中国城
   London city center Chinatown

5. C 普通话
   Mandarin

CHAPTER 10

几句有意思的中文 – SEVERAL INTERESTING CHINESE SENTENCES

学习**外语**是一件很有意思的事情。你可以听到不同的**发音**，可以学到怎么样把**词连**在一起说成**句子**。你还会学到一些不同的文化，**通过**文化之间的**对比**，你可以很**清楚**地看到不同文化对事情的不同**看法**。

今天我们就来看一看几句**常用**的中文。你可能已经听到过，可是它们的**意思**可能不是你**想象**的那样，或者你不明白中文为什么这么说？

中文里有个词语叫"老小孩儿"，很多外国人都很不**理解**。他们觉得这个词**错**了，他们觉得**如果**是小孩儿，怎么会是老呢？其实中文的意思是说人老了有时候跟小孩儿一样，**容易高兴**，也容易**生气**。现在**明白**了吗？

在中国，去朋友家玩儿，离开时朋友可能对你说"慢走"，很多外国人觉得很**奇怪**，不明白**真正**的**含义**，其实中国人的意思是让你在回去的路上小心点儿，不是让你慢点儿走。你可能还听主人说过"保重"，这个词**表面**的意思是说"**保持体重**"。你可能也不理解，为什么中国人说"保持体重"？现在的人都想**瘦**一点儿，**苗条**一点儿。中国人**认为**如果人很**辛苦**，很累，就会瘦的，所以"保重"的意思是让你自己好好**照顾**自己，不要瘦了，要保持体重。

外国人学习中文时，如果你对他们说"你中文说得很好。"大多数的时候，他们都会说"谢谢！"如果你碰到一个**中国通**，你会听到"哪里哪里！"或者"**你过奖了！**"不同的**回答体现**了不同的文化。在西方，如果你**夸赞**一个人或者一件事，对方的回答常常会是"谢谢！"可是中国人认为**谦虚**是**美德**，中国人的回答往往是"哪里哪里！"哪里哪里的表面意思是在哪儿，在这里是表示谦虚。看来一个国家的文化和它的语言**的确**是很有**关系**的。

几句有意思的中文– Several Interesting Chinese Sentences With English Translation

学习**外语**是一件很有意思的事情。你可以听到不同的**发音**，可以学到怎么样把**词**连在一起说成**句子**。

Xuéxí **wàiyǔ** shì yíjiàn hěn yǒuyìsi de shìqing. Nǐ kěyǐ tīng dào bùtóng de **fāyīn**, kěyǐ xué dào zěnme yàng bǎ **cí** lián zài yìqǐ shuō chéng **jùzi**.

Learning a **foreign language** is very interesting. You can hear different **pronunciations** and learn how to put **words** together into **sentences**.

你还会学到一些不同的文化，**通过**文化**之间**的**对比**，你可以很**清楚**地看到不同文化对事情的不同**看法**。

Nǐ hái huì xué dào yìxiē bùtóng de wénhuà, **tōngguò** wénhuà **zhījiān** de **duìbǐ**, nǐ kěyǐ hěn **qīngchǔ** de kàn dào bùtóng wénhuà duì shìqing de bùtóng **kànfǎ**.

You will also learn about different cultures, and **through** the **contrast between** cultures, you can see very **clearly** how different cultures **view** things differently.

今天我们就来看一看几句**常用**的中文。你可能已经听到过，可是它们的**意思**可能不是你**想象**的那样，或者你不明白中文为什么这么说。

Jīntiān wǒmen jiù lái kàn yi kàn jǐ jù **chángyòng** de Zhōngwén. Nǐ kěnéng yǐjīng tīng dàoguò, kěshì tāmen de **yìsi** kěnéng búshì nǐ **xiǎngxiàng** de nàyàng, huòzhě nǐ bù míngbai Zhōngwén wèishénme zhème shuō.

Today we will take a look at some **commonly used** Chinese sentences. You may have heard them, but they may not **mean** what

124

you **imagined**, or you do not understand why Chinese people say it this way.

中文里有个词语叫"老小孩儿"，很多外国人都很不**理解**。他们觉得这个词**错**了，他们觉得**如果**是小孩儿，怎么会是老呢？

Zhōngwén lǐ yǒu gè cíyǔ jiào "lǎo xiǎoháir", hěnduō wàiguó rén dōu hěn bù **lǐjiě**. Tāmen juéde zhège cí cuòle, tāmen juéde **rúguǒ** shì xiǎoháir, zěnme huì shì lǎo ne?

There is a word in Chinese meaning "old child", which many foreigners do not **understand**. They feel that the word is **wrong**; they feel that **if** it is a child, how can s/he be old?

其实中文的意思是说人老了有时候跟小孩儿一样，**容易高兴**，也容易**生气**。现在**明白**了吗！

Qíshí Zhōngwén de yìsi shì shuō rén lǎole yǒu shíhou gēn xiǎoháir yíyàng, **róngyì gāoxìng**, yě róngyì **shēngqì**. Xiànzài **míngbai**le ma?

In fact, the meaning in Chinese is to say that when people are old, sometimes they are like children. They are **easy** to make **happy** and easy to make **angry**. **Get it** now?

在中国，去朋友家玩儿，离开时朋友可能对你说"慢走"，很多外国人觉得很**奇怪**，不明白**真正**的**含义**，其实中国人的意思是让你在回去的路上小心点儿，不是让你慢点儿走。

Zài Zhōngguó, qù péngyǒu jiā wánr, líkāi shí péngyǒu kěnéng duì nǐ shuō "màn zǒu", hěnduō wàiguó rén juéde hěn **qíguài**, bù míngbái **zhēnzhèng** de **hányì**, qíshí Zhōngguó rén de yìsi shì ràng nǐ zài huíqù de lùshàng xiǎoxīn diǎnr, búshì ràng nǐ màn diǎnr zǒu.

In China, when you go to a friend's house to visit, your friend may say "walk slowly" to you as you are leaving. Many foreigners find it **strange** and don't understand the **real meaning**. In fact, the Chinese mean that you should be careful on the way back; they're not asking you to go slow.

你可能还听主人说过"保重"，这个词**表面**的意思是说 **"保持体重"**。你可能也不理解，为什么中国人说"保持体重"？

Nǐ kěnéng hái tīng zhǔrén shuō guò "bǎozhòng", zhège cí **biǎomiàn** de yìsi shì shuō "**Bǎochí tǐzhòng**". Nǐ kěnéng yě bù lǐjiě, wèishénme Zhōngguó rén shuō "bǎochí tǐzhòng"?

You may also have heard your host say "take care", which **literally** translates to "**maintain your weight**". You may also not understand, why do the Chinese say "keep your weight"?

现在的人都想**瘦**一点儿，**苗条**一点儿。中国人**认为**如果人很**辛苦**，很累，就会瘦的，所以"保重"的意思是让你自己好好**照顾**自己，不要瘦了，要保持体重。

Xiànzài de rén dōu xiǎng **shòu** yīdiǎnr, **miáotiao** yìdiǎnr. Zhōngguó rén rènwéi rúguǒ rén hěn **xīnkǔ**, hěn lèi, jiù huì shòu de, suǒyǐ "bǎozhòng" de yìsi shì ràng nǐ zìjǐ hǎohao **zhàogù** zìjǐ, búyào shòule, yào bǎochí tǐzhòng.

People nowadays want to be **thinner** and **slimmer**. Chinese people **think** that if people **work hard** and are tired, they will lose weight, so "take care" asks you to **take good care of** yourself, don't lose weight, keep your weight.

外国人学习中文时，如果你对他们说"你中文说得很好。"大多数的时候，他们都会说"谢谢！"如果你碰到一个**中国通**，你会听到"哪里哪里！"或者"**你过奖了！**"不同的**回答体现**了不同的文化。

Wàiguó rén xuéxí Zhōngwén shí, rúguǒ nǐ duì tāmen shuō "Nǐ Zhōngwén shuō dé hěn hǎo." Dàduōshǔ de shíhou, tāmen dōu huì shuō "xièxie!" Rúguǒ nǐ pèng dào yígè **Zhōngguó tōng**, nǐ huì tīng dào "Nǎlǐ nǎlǐ!" Huòzhě "**Nǐ guòjiǎngle**!" Bùtóng de **huídá tǐxiàn** le bùtóng de wénhuà.

When a foreigner is learning Chinese, if you say to them "You speak Chinese very well," most of the time they will say "Thank you!" If you meet a **foreigner who knows Chinese and China well**, you will hear "Where where!" or **"You have overpraised!"** Different **responses reflect** different cultures.

在西方，如果你**夸赞**一个人或者一件事，对方的回答常常会是"谢谢！"可是中国人认为**谦虚**是**美德**，中国人的回答往往是"哪里哪里！"哪里哪里的表面意思是在哪儿，在这里是表示谦虚。

Zài Xīfāng, rúguǒ nǐ **kuāzàn** yígè rén huòzhě yíjiàn shì, duìfāng de huídá chángcháng huì shì "Xièxie!" Kěshì Zhōngguó rén rènwéi **qiānxū** shì **měidé**, Zhōngguó rén de huídá wǎngwǎng shì "Nǎlǐ nǎlǐ!" Nǎlǐ nǎlǐ de biǎomiàn yìsi shì zài nǎr, zài zhèlǐ shì biǎoshì qiānxū.

In the West, if you **compliment** someone or something, the other person's answer is often "Thank you!" But the Chinese believe that **modesty** is a **virtue**, and the Chinese answer is often "Where where?" The superficial meaning is where, but in this context it is an expression of modesty.

看来一个国家的文化和它的语言**的确**是很有**关系**的。

Kàn lái yígè guójiā de wénhuà hé tā de yǔyán **díquè** shì hěn yǒu **guānxì** de.

It seems that a country's culture and its language are **indeed** closely **related**.

总结/Summary

学习外语是一件很有意思的事情。你可以听到新的发音，学习怎么样把词连在一起说成句子，还可以学到不同的文化。通过文化之间的对比，你可以理解不同文化对事情不同的看法。中文里有一个词"老小孩儿"，很多人觉得小孩儿怎么会老呢？这个词是说人老了，有时候跟小孩一样，容易高兴，也容易生气。在中国，去朋友家做客，走的时候主人会说"慢走"，主人不是让你慢慢走，主人的意思是让你在路上小心点儿。有时候主人也会说"保重"，他们的意思是让你自己好好照顾自己。文化也会在语言中体现出来。如果你夸赞西方人，他们常常会说"谢谢"。中国人就不同了，他们会说"哪里哪里？"，表面的意思是在哪儿，在这里是表示谦虚。

Xuéxí wàiyǔ shì yíjiàn hěn yǒuyìsi de shìqing. Nǐ kěyǐ tīng dào xīn de fā yīn, xuéxí zěnme yàng bǎ cí lián zài yìqǐ shuō chéng jùzi, hái kěyǐ xué dào bùtóng de wénhuà. tōngguò wénhuà zhījiān de duìbǐ, nǐ kěyǐ lǐjiě bùtóng wénhuà duì shìqing bùtóng de kànfǎ. Zhōngwén lǐ yǒu yígè cí"lǎo xiǎoháir", hěnduō rén juéde xiǎoháir zěnme huì lǎo ne? Zhège cí shì shuō rén lǎole, yǒu shíhou gēn xiǎohái yíyàng, róngyì gāoxìng, yě róngyì shēngqì. Zài Zhōngguó, qù péngyǒu jiā zuòkè, zǒu de shíhou zhǔrén huì shuō"màn zǒu", zhǔrén búshì ràng nǐ màn man zǒu, zhǔrén de yìsi shì ràng nǐ zài lùshàng xiǎoxīn diǎnr. Yǒu shíhou zhǔrén yě huì shuō"bǎozhòng", tāmen de yìsi shì ràng nǐ zìjǐ hǎohao zhàogù zìjǐ. Wénhuà yě huì zài yǔyán zhōng tǐxiàn chūlái. Rúguǒ nǐ kuāzàn Xīfāng rén, tāmen chángcháng huì shuō "Xièxiè". Zhōngguó rén jiù bùtóngle, tāmen huì shuō"Nǎlǐ nǎlǐ?", biǎomiàn de yìsi shì zài nǎr, zài zhèlǐ shì biǎoshì qiānxū.

Learning a foreign language is very interesting. You can hear new sounds, learn how to put words together into sentences, and you can learn about different cultures, and by comparing cultures, you can understand how different cultures view things differently. There is a word in Chinese, "old child", and many people think how can a child be old? This word means that when people are old, sometimes they are like children, easily happy and easily angry. In China, when you go to a friend's house as a guest, the host will say "walk slowly" when you leave. They are asking you to walk carefully, not walk slowly. Sometimes hosts will also say "maintain weight" to ask you to take good care of yourself. Culture is also reflected in language. If you compliment Westerners, they often say "thank you". The Chinese are different. They will say "Where where?" or "You have overpraised!" The superficial meaning is where where, but it is an expression of modesty.

生词/Vocabulary List

- **外语** – wàiyǔ: foreign language
- **发音** – fāyīn: to pronounce, pronunciation
- **词** – cí: word
- **连** – lián: to connect
- **句子** – jùzi: sentence
- **通过** – tōngguò: through
- **之间** – zhījiān: between
- **对比** – duìbǐ: to compare, to be compared with
- **清楚** – qīngchǔ: clear
- **看法** – kànfǎ: viewpoint
- **常用** – chángyòng: commonly used
- **意思** – yìsi: meaning
- **想象** – xiǎngxiàng: to imagine
- **理解** – lǐjiě: to understand
- **错** – cuò: wrong
- **如果** – rúguǒ: if
- **容易** – róngyì: easy
- **高兴** – gāoxìng: happy
- **生气** – shēngqì: angry
- **明白** – míngbai: to understand, to be clear
- **奇怪** – qíguài: strange
- **真正** – zhēnzhèng: real
- **含义** – hányì: meaning
- **保持** – bǎochí: to maintain
- **体重** – tǐzhòng: weight
- **瘦** – shòu: thin, lean
- **苗条** – miáotiao: slim
- **认为** – rènwéi: to believe, to think
- **辛苦** – xīnkǔ: to work hard
- **照顾** – zhàogù: to take care of
- **中国通** – Zhōngguó tōng: foreigner who knows Chinese and China well
- **过奖** – guòjiǎng: to overpraise
- **回答** – huídá: to reply
- **体现** – tǐxiàn: to reflect
- **夸赞** – kuāzàn: to praise
- **谦虚** – qiānxū: modesty
- **美德** – měidé: virtue
- **的确** – díquè: indeed
- **关系** – guānxì: relation

问题 / **Questions**

1. 学习外语是一件很无聊的事情。

   Learning a foreign language is very boring.

   A. 对
   B. 错

2. 学习外语时，你不可以学到它的文化。

   When learning a foreign language, you can't learn about its culture.

   A. 对
   B. 错

3. 主人说"慢走"的意思是让你在回家的路上小心点儿。

   When the host says "walk slowly", it means to be careful on the way home.

   A. 对
   B. 错

4. 主人说"保重"的意思是让你好好照顾自己。

   When the host says "maintain weight", it means that you take good care of yourself.

   A. 对
   B. 错

5. 文化和语言是没有关系的。

   Culture and language are not related.

   A. 对
   B. 错

答案/Answers

1. B 错
   False

2. B 错
   False

3. A 对
   True

4. A 对
   True

5. B 错
   False

CHAPTER 11

小狗皮帕 – PUPPY PIPPA

皮帕是一只**讨人喜爱**的小狗。她的**主人**是**芭芭拉**和**理查德**，一对**退休**的英国**夫妇**。他们住在英国伦敦**东南**的一**幢**大房子里。

芭芭拉退休前是小学音乐老师，她是十年前退的休。理查德退休还要早一些，他十五年前就退休了。芭芭拉一直都想**养**一条**宠物**狗，可是当老师的时候，她的工作非常忙，所以直到她退休以后才**如愿以偿**。

皮帕是芭芭拉和理查德在一家宠物店买的。芭芭拉第一眼看到皮帕就喜欢上她了，**当天**就把她买下来，带回家了。皮帕那时才八个星期大，她好小好瘦啊！把皮帕带回家的当天，理查德就先开车到**超市**买了一些小狗吃的**饼干**和牛奶，然后又到了一个很大的宠物店买了一些小狗**需要**的**用品**，比如说：**洗头膏、沐浴露、毛巾、垫子、玩具**和**笼子**等等。宠物店还给了芭芭拉一件 **T 恤衫**，T 恤衫上有皮帕妈妈的**气味**。理查德把垫子、玩具和笼子放在厨房的一个**角落**里，这就是皮帕的家。角落在门旁边，门外面就是花园。**接下来**的一两个星期，芭芭拉和理查德对皮帕**进行了如厕训练**。

一天一天地小皮帕开始**长大**，慢慢地她也胖了一点儿。理查德每天早上六点起床，起床后的第一件事就是带皮帕到外面**散步**。理查德和芭芭拉的房子在**泰晤士河边**，理查德**牵**着小皮帕顺着河边走一个小时。每天散步的时候，都会看到**别**的小狗，皮帕总是**不停**地**朝**它们**叫**，很**凶**的**样子**。晚饭后，芭芭拉和理查德坐在电视机前面看电视，皮帕总是喜欢坐在芭芭拉的**腿**上。**如果芭芭拉躺**在沙发上，皮帕就在芭芭拉身上走来走去**直到**累了，然后就躺在芭芭拉**脖子**边**休息**休息。

皮帕是一只**被惯坏**了的小狗。芭芭拉不知道给她买了多少**套**漂亮的**狗装**。芭芭拉总是说：皮帕想要什么我们就给她什么。

小狗皮帕 – Puppy Pippa
With English Translation

皮帕是一只**讨人喜爱**的小狗。她的**主人**是**芭芭拉**和**理查德**，一对**退休**的英国**夫妇**。他们住在英国伦敦**东南**的一**幢**大房子里。

Pípà shì yì zhī **tǎo rén xǐ'ài** de xiǎo gǒu. Tā de **zhǔrén** shì **Bābālā** hé **Lǐchádé**, yí **duì tuìxiū** de Yīngguó **fūfù**. Tāmen zhù zài Yīngguó Lúndūn **dōngnán** de yí **zhuàng** dà fángzi lǐ.

Pippa is an **endearing** puppy. Her **owners** are **Barbara** and **Richard**, a **retired** British **couple**. They live in **a** large house in **southeast** London, England.

芭芭拉退休前是小学音乐老师，她是十年前退的休。理查德退休还要早一些，他十五年前就退休了。

Bābālā tuìxiū qián shì xiǎoxué yīnyuè lǎoshī, tā shì shí nián qián tuì de xiū. Lǐchádé tuìxiū hái yào zǎo yìxiē, tā shíwǔ nián qián jiù tuìxiūle.

Barbara was a primary school music teacher before retiring; she retired ten years ago. Richard retired even earlier; he retired fifteen years ago.

芭芭拉一直都想**养**一条**宠物**狗，可是当老师的时候，她的工作非常忙，所以直到她退休以后才**如愿以偿**。

Bābālā yìzhí dōu xiǎng **yǎng** yìtiáo **chǒngwù** gǒu, kěshì dāng lǎoshī de shíhou, tā de gōngzuò fēicháng máng, suǒyǐ zhídào tā tuìxiū yǐhòu cái **rúyuànyǐcháng**.

Barbara has always wanted to **raise** a **pet** dog, but she was so busy as a teacher that she couldn't **fulfill her wish** until she retired.

皮帕是芭芭拉和理查德在一家宠物店买的。芭芭拉第一眼看到皮帕就喜欢上她了，**当天**就把她买下来，带回家了。皮帕那时才八个星期大，她好小好瘦啊！

Pípà shì Bābālā hé Lǐchádé zài yìjiā chǒngwù diàn mǎi de. Bābālā dìyī yǎn kàn dào Pípà jiù xǐhuān shàng tāle, **dāngtiān** jiù bǎ tā mǎi xiàlái, dài huíjiāle. Pípà nà shí cái bā gè xīngqī dà, tā hǎo xiǎo hǎo shòu a!

Pippa was bought by Barbara and Richard at a pet store. Barbara fell in love with Pippa at first sight; she bought her **on the same day** and took her home. Pippa was only eight weeks old, and she was so small and skinny!

把皮帕带回家的当天，理查德就先开车到**超市**买了一些小狗吃的**饼干**和牛奶，然后又到了一个很大的宠物店买了一些小狗**需要**的**用品**，比如说：**洗头膏、沐浴露、毛巾、垫子、玩具**和**笼子**等等。

Bǎ Pípà dài huíjiā de dāngtiān, Lǐchádé jiù xiān kāichē dào **chāoshì** mǎile yìxiē xiǎo gǒu chī de **bǐnggān** hé niúnǎi, ránhòu yòu dàole yígè hěn dà de chǒngwù diàn mǎile yìxiē xiǎo gǒu **xūyào** de **yòngpǐn**, bǐrú shuō: **xǐ tóu gāo, mùyù lù, máojīn, diànzi, wánjù** hé **lóngzi** děng děng.

On the day they brought Pippa home, Richard first drove to the **supermarket** to buy some **biscuits** and milk for the puppy, and then went to a large pet store to buy some **supplies** the puppy **needed**, such as: **shampoo, shower gel, towels, mats, toys** and **cages**, among other items.

宠物店还给了芭芭拉一件 **T 恤衫**，T 恤衫上有皮帕妈妈的**气味**。理查德把垫子，玩具和笼子放在厨房的一个**角落**里，这就是皮帕的家。角落在门旁边，门外面就是花园。

Chǒngwù diàn hái gěile Bābālā yíjiàn **T xùshān**, T xùshān shàng yǒu Pípà māma de **qìwèi**. Lǐchádé bǎ diànzi, wánjù hé lóngzi fàng zài chúfáng de yígè **jiǎoluò** lǐ, zhè jiùshì Pípà de jiā. Jiǎoluò zài mén pángbiān, mén wàimiàn jiùshì huāyuán.

The pet store also gave Barbara a **T-shirt** that has the **scent** of Pippa's mother. Richard keeps cushions, toys and a cage in a **corner** of the kitchen, which is Pippa's home. The corner is next to the door, and outside the door is the garden.

接下来的一两个星期，芭芭拉和理查德对皮帕**进行**了**如厕训练**。

Jiē xiàlái de yì liǎnggè xīngqī, Bābālā hé Lǐchádé duì Pípà **jìnxíng** le **rú cè xùnliàn**.

For **the following** week or two, Barbara and Richard **toilet-trained** Pippa.

一天一天地小皮帕开始**长大**，慢慢地她也胖了一点儿。

Yìtiān yìtiān de xiǎo Pípà kāishǐ **zhǎng dà**, màn man de tā yě pàngle yìdiǎnr.

Day by day, little Pippa began to **grow**, and slowly she also gained a little weight.

理查德每天早上六点起床，起床后的第一件事就是带皮帕到外面**散步**。理查德和芭芭拉的房子在**泰晤士河边**，理查德**牵**着小皮帕**顺**着河边走一个小时。

Lǐchádé měitiān zǎoshang liù diǎn qǐchuáng, qǐchuáng hòu de dìyī jiàn shì jiùshì dài Pípà dào wàimiàn **sànbù**. Lǐchádé hé Bābālā de fángzi zài **Tàiwùshìhé biān**, Lǐchádé **qiān**zhe xiǎo Pípà **shùn**zhe hé biān zǒu yígè xiǎoshí.

Richard wakes up at six every morning, and the first thing he does after waking up is to take Pippa for a **walk** outside. Richard and Barbara's house is by **the River Thames**, and Richard **leads** and walks little Pippa **along** the river for an hour.

每天散步的时候，都会看到**别**的小狗，皮帕总是**不停**地**朝**它们**叫**，很**凶**的样子。

Měitiān sànbù de shíhou, dōu huì kàn dào **bié** de xiǎo gǒu, Pípà zǒngshì **bù tíng** de **cháo** tāmen jiào, hěn **xiōng** de **yàngzi**.

When walking every day, Pippa sees **other** puppies, and she **barks** at them nonstop, looking **fierce**.

晚饭后，芭芭拉和理查德坐在电视机前面看电视，皮帕总是喜欢坐在芭芭拉的**腿**上。**如果**芭芭拉**躺**在沙发上，皮帕就在芭芭拉身上走来走去**直到**累了，然后就躺在芭芭拉**脖子**边**休息**休息。

Wǎnfàn hòu, Bābālā hé Lǐchádé zuò zài diànshìjī qiánmiàn kàn diànshì, Pípà zǒngshì xǐhuān zuò zài Bābālā de **tuǐ** shàng. **Rúguǒ** Bābālā **tǎng** zài shāfā shàng, Pípá jiù zài Bābālā shēnshang zǒu lái zǒu qù **zhídào** lèile, ránhòu jiù **tǎng** zài Bābālā **bózi** biān **xiūxi** xiūxi.

After dinner, Barbara and Richard sit watching TV, and Pippa always likes to sit on Barbara's **lap**. **If** Barbara **lies** on the sofa, Pippa just walks up and down on Barbara **until** she is tired, and then lies on the side of Barbara's **neck** to **rest** a bit.

皮帕是一只**被惯坏**了的小狗。芭芭拉不知道给她买了多少**套**漂亮的**狗装**。芭芭拉总是说：皮帕想要什么我们就给她什么。

Pípà shì yìzhī **bèi guàn huài**le de xiǎo gǒu. Bābālā bù zhīdào gěi tā mǎile duōshǎo **tào** piàoliang de **gǒu zhuāng**. Bābālā zǒngshì shuō: Pípà xiǎng yào shénme wǒmen jiù gěi tā shénme.

Pippa is a **spoiled** puppy. Barbara doesn't know how many beautiful **dog suits** she's bought for her. Barbara always says: We'll give Pippa whatever she wants.

总结/Summary

皮帕是芭芭拉和理查德的宠物狗。他们是从一家宠物店把皮帕买回来的。芭芭拉一直都想养一条宠物狗，可是因为以前工作忙，所以直到退休后她才有了皮帕。皮帕刚来的时候又小又瘦，慢慢地它开始长大长胖。每天早上理查德带皮帕出去散步。晚饭后，皮帕总是喜欢坐在芭芭拉的腿上或者躺在芭芭拉脖子边休息。皮帕是一只被惯坏了的小狗。芭芭拉给她买了很多套漂亮的狗装。芭芭拉总是说：皮帕想要什么我们就给她什么。

Pípà shì Bābālā hé Lǐchádé de chǒngwù gǒu. Tāmen shì cóng yìjiā chǒngwù diàn bǎ Pípà mǎi huílái de. Bābālā yìzhí dōu xiǎng yǎng yìtiáo chǒngwù gǒu, kěshì yīnwèi yǐqián gōngzuò máng, suǒyǐ zhí dào tuìxiū hòu tā cái yǒule Pípà. Pípà gāng lái de shíhou yòu xiǎo yòu shòu, màn man de tā kāishǐ zhǎng dà zhǎng pàng. Měitiān zǎoshang Lǐchádé dài Pípà chūqù sànbù. Wǎnfàn hòu, Pípà zǒngshì xǐhuān zuò zài Bābālā de tuǐ shàng huòzhě tǎng zài Bābālā bózi biān xiūxi. Pípà shì yìzhī bèi guàn huàile de xiǎo gǒu. Bābālā gěi tā mǎile hěnduō tào piàoliang de gǒu zhuāng. Bābālā zǒngshì shuō: Pípà xiǎng yào shénme wǒmen jiù gěi tā shénme.

Pippa is Barbara and Richard's pet dog. They got Pippa from a pet store. Barbara has always wanted to have a dog, but because of her busy work, she only got Pippa after retirement. Pippa was small and thin when she first arrived, but slowly she started to grow and gain weight. Every morning Richard takes Pippa out for a walk. After dinner, Pippa always likes to sit on Barbara's lap or lie on Barbara's neck to rest. Pippa is a spoiled puppy. Barbara bought her a lot of beautiful dog clothes. Barbara always says: We'll give Pippa whatever she wants.

生词/Vocabulary List

- 讨人喜爱 – tǎo rén xǐ'ài: endearing
- 主人 – zhǔrén: owner
- 对 – duì: pair
- 退休 – tuìxiū: to retire
- 夫妇 – fūfù: couple
- 东南 – dōngnán: southeast
- 幢 – zhuàng: measure word for a building of two or more stories
- 养 – yǎng: to raise
- 宠物 – chǒngwù: pet
- 如愿以偿 – rúyuànyǐcháng: to get one's wish
- 当天 – dāngtiān: on the day
- 超市 – chāoshì: supermarket
- 饼干 – bǐnggān: biscuit
- 需要 – xūyào: to need
- 用品 – yòngpǐn: supplies
- 洗头膏 – xǐ tóu gāo: shampoo
- 沐浴露 – mùyù lù: shower gel
- 毛巾 – máojīn: towel
- 垫子 – diànzi: mat
- 玩具 – wánjù: toy
- 笼子 – lóngzi: pet crate
- T 恤衫 – T xù shān: T-shirt
- 气味 – qìwèi: scent
- 角落 – jiǎoluò: corner
- 接下来 - jiē xiàlái: the following, next
- 进行 – jìnxíng: to carry out, to do
- 如厕训练 – rú cè xùnliàn: to toilet train, toilet training
- 长大 – zhǎng dà: to grow up
- 散步 – sànbù: to walk
- 泰晤士河 – Tàiwùshìhé: River Thames
- 边 – biān: side
- 牵 – qiān: to lead along
- 顺 – shùn: along
- 不停 – bù tíng: nonstop
- 朝 – cháo: towards
- 叫 – jiào: to bark, to shout
- 凶 – xiōng: fierce
- 腿 – tuǐ: leg
- 如果 – rúguǒ : if
- 躺 – tǎng : to lie down
- 直到 – zhídào: until
- 脖子 – bózi : neck
- 休息 – xiūxi : to rest

- 被惯坏 – bèi guàn huài: spoiled
- 套 – tào : set, measure word for clothes
- 狗装 – gǒu zhuāng : dog clothes

问题/Questions

1. 芭芭拉以前工作的时候就有了皮帕。

   Barbara got Pippa while she was working as a teacher.

   A. 对
   B. 错

2. 芭芭拉和理查德住在英国伦敦的东南。

   Barbara and Richard live in southeast London, England.

   A. 对
   B. 错

3. 理查德从超市买了什么？

   What did Richard buy from the supermarket?

   A. 饼干
   B. 洗发膏
   C. 垫子
   D. T恤衫

4. 芭芭拉每天早上带皮帕去散步。

   Barbara takes Pippa for a walk every morning.

   A. 对
   B. 错

5. 皮帕现在和以前一样瘦。

   Pippa is now as thin as ever.

   A. 对
   B. 错

答案/Answers

1. B 错
   False

2. A 对
   True

3. A 饼干
   biscuits

4. B 错
   False

5. B 错
   False

CHAPTER 12

艾米六年的大学生活 –
AMY'S SIX YEARS OF UNI LIFE

大学**时代**是人一生中的**黄金年华**。高中时期一个又一个的**考试**都成了昨天，**压力小了**，**自由多了**，可以**追求**自己的**梦想**，努力地**提高**自己。**苏格兰**女孩艾米的大学**经历**就很**酷**！

十八岁那年艾米接到了**思克莱德**大学的**录取通知书**，她好**激动**！还是个小女孩的时候，艾米就**展现**出了**过人的语言天赋**。她喜欢**模仿**不同地方和国家的口音。等到她上**初中**的时候，学生们可以**选择**一门外语，艾米选择了**西班牙语**。以后的几年里，在西班牙语课上，艾米**如鱼得水**，课程对她来说太简单了。

很**自然地**艾米上大学的时候选择了**主修**西班牙文和**意大利文**。她的**课程**一共是五年。在苏格兰，**学士学位**一般只要三年。**之所以**艾米要五年时间才能**毕业**，是因为她学的是语言**专业**，她要选择到说西班牙文和意大利文的国家各**实习一年**。

艾米选择了意大利的**维罗纳**大学。维罗纳城是**联合国教科文组织世界遗产**。艾米很喜欢那里的**中世纪的广场**、**喷泉**和**建筑**，**更不要提**意大利的**美食**了！在维罗纳大学的一年，艾米在大学的英语学院教英语。来学英语的学生很多都是**初学者**，一句英文也不会说。艾米学到了很多教外语的**技能**，同时也大大地提高了她自己的意大利文。

艾米从上初中就开始学西班牙文，所以当选择到哪个大学去进一步提高自己的西班牙文时，艾米**决定大胆**一些，她没有选择西班牙，她决定到**南美洲**的**厄瓜多尔**去。这次她去了一个很小的大学，这个大学在**安第斯山区**。在那一年里，她**接触**到了很多厄瓜多尔安第斯山区的**土著**孩子们，那一年给艾米**留下**了很多**美好**的**记忆**。

值得一提的是：艾米大三的时候，学院告诉学生们，他们如果想学中文，可以到中国的**天津外国语大学**学习一年。艾米知道这个**机会**很**难得**。近十年来，越来越多的人开始学习中

文，所以艾米选择了这个机会。到了天津以后，艾米才知道中文有多难，而且中国的文化

和西方文化的**差异**又很大，所以这一年对艾米来说太难了！头三个月，艾米只会说几句中文，三个月以后，她可以自己买东西，可还是很难。艾米在天津一共住了九个月，直到最后的一两个月她才开始觉得中文不那么难了！

现在艾米常常回想起自己六年的大学生活，**说起来**六年是很长的时间，可是自己那六年的大学过得好快啊！

艾米六年的大学生活 – Amy's Six Years of Uni Life
With English Translation

大学时代是人一生中的**黄金年华**。高中时期一个又一个的**考试**都成了昨天，**压力**小了，**自由**多了，可以**追求**自己的**梦想**，**努力**地**提高**自己。苏格兰女孩艾米的大学**经历**就很**酷**！

Dàxué **shídài** shì rén yìshēng zhōng de **huángjīn niánhuá**. Gāozhōng shíqí yígè yòu yígè de **kǎoshì** dōu chéngle zuótiān, **yālì** xiǎole, **zìyóu** duōle, kěyǐ **zhuīqiú** zìjǐ de **mèngxiǎng**, **nǔlì** de **tígāo** zìjǐ. **Sūgélán** nǚhái Àimǐ de dàxué **jīnglì** jiù hěn kù!

The university **years** are the **golden years** of a person's life. One **test** after another in high school is a thing of the past. With less **pressure** and more **freedom**, you can **pursue** your **dreams** and **work hard** to **improve** yourself. Amy, a girl from **Scotland**, had a **cool** uni **experience**.

十八岁那年艾米接到了**思克莱德**大学的**录取通知书**，她好**激动**！还是个小女孩的时候，艾米就**展现**出了**过人**的**语言天赋**。她喜欢**模仿**不同地方和国家的**口音**。

Shíbā suì nà nián Àimǐ jiē dàole **Sīkèláidé** dàxué de **lùqǔ tōngzhīshū**, tā hǎo **jīdòng**! Háishì gè xiǎo nǚhái de shíhou, Àimǐ jiù **zhǎnxiàn** chūle **guò rén** de **yǔyán tiānfù**. Tā xǐhuān **mófǎng** bùtóng dìfāng hé guójiā de **kǒuyīn**.

At the age of eighteen, Amy received an **offer** from the **University of Strathclyde**. She was so **excited**! As a little girl, Amy already **showed** an **extraordinary talent** for **languages**. She likes to **imitate** the **accents** of different places and countries.

等到她上**初中**的时候，学生们可以**选择**一门外语，艾米选择了**西班牙语**。以后的几年里，在西班牙语课上，艾米**如鱼得水**，课程对她来说太简单了。

Děngdào tā shàng **chūzhōng** de shíhou, xuéshēngmen kěyǐ **xuǎnzé** yì mén wàiyǔ, Àimǐ xuǎnzéle **Xībānyáyǔ**. Yǐhòu de jǐ nián lǐ, zài Xībānyáyǔ kè shàng, Àimǐ **rúyúdéshuǐ**, kèchéng duì tā lái shuō tài jiǎndānle.

By the time she entered **secondary school**, students could **choose** a foreign language, and Amy chose **Spanish**. For the next few years, Amy felt like **a fish in water** in Spanish classes: the coursework was too easy for her.

很**自然地**艾米上大学的时候选择了**主修**西班牙文和**意大利文**。她的**课程**一共是五年。在苏格兰，**学士学位**一般只要三年。

Hěn **zìrán de** Àimǐ shàng dàxué de shíhou xuǎnzéle **zhǔ xiū** Xībānyáwén hé **Yìdàlìwén**. Tā de **kèchéng** yígòng shì wǔ nián. Zài Sūgélán, **xuéshì xuéwèi** yībān zhǐ yào sān nián.

Naturally, Amy chose to **major in** Spanish and **Italian** when she went to uni. Her **studies** are five years in total. In Scotland, a **Bachelor's degree** generally only takes three years.

之所以艾米要五年时间才能**毕业**，是因为她学的是语言**专业**，她要选择到说西班牙文和意大利文的国家各**实习**一年。

Zhī suǒyǐ Àimǐ yào wǔ nián shíjiān cái néng **bìyè**, shì yīnwèi tā xué de shì yǔyán **zhuānyè**, tā yào xuǎnzé dào shuō Xībānyáwén hé Yìdàlìwén de guójiā gè **shíxí** yì nián.

The reason why Amy took five years to **graduate** is because she **majored** in languages, and she needed to do a one-year **internship** in a country where Spanish and Italian, respectively, were spoken.

艾米选择了意大利的**维罗纳**大学。维罗纳城是**联合国教科文组织世界遗产**。艾米很喜欢那里的**中世纪**的**广场**，**喷泉**和**建筑**，**更不要提**意大利的**美食**了！

Àimǐ xuǎnzéle Yìdàlì de **Wéiluónà** Dàxué. Wéiluōnàchéng shì **Liánhéguó Jiàokēwén Zǔzhī Shìjiè Yíchǎn**. Àimǐ hěn xǐhuān nàlǐ de **zhōngshìjì** de **guǎngchǎng**, **pēnquán** hé **jiànzhù**, **gèng búyào tí** Yìdàlì de **měishí** le!

Amy chose the **University of Verona** in Italy. The city of Verona is a **UNESCO World Heritage Site**. Amy loves the **medieval squares**, **fountains** and **architecture**, **not to mention** the Italian **food**!

在维罗纳大学的一年，艾米在大学的英语学院教英语。来学英语的学生很多都是**初学者**，一句英文也不会说。艾米学到了很多教外语的**技能**，同时也大大地提高了她自己的意大利文。

Zài Wéiluónà Dàxué de yì nián, Àimǐ zài dàxué de yīngyǔ xuéyuàn jiāo Yīngyǔ. Lái xué Yīngyǔ de xuéshēng hěnduō dōu shì **chū xué zhě**, yíjù Yīngwén yě bú huì shuō. Àimǐ xué dàole hěnduō jiāo wàiyǔ de **jìnéng**, tóngshí yě dàdà de tígāole tā zìjǐ de Yìdàlìwén.

During her year at the University of Verona, Amy taught English at the University's English Faculty. Many students who come to learn English are **beginners** and cannot speak a word of English. Amy has learned many **skills** in teaching foreign languages, while also improving her Italian greatly.

艾米从上初中就开始学西班牙文，所以当选择到哪个大学去进一步提高自己的西班牙文时，艾米**决定大胆**一些，她没有选择西班牙，她决定到**南美洲**的厄瓜多尔去。

Àimǐ cóng shàng chūzhōng jiù kāishǐ xué Xībānyáwén, suǒyǐ dāng xuǎnzé dào nǎge dàxué qù jìn yí bù tígāo zìjǐ de Xībānyáwén shí, Àimǐ **juédìng dàdǎn** yìxiē, tā méiyǒu xuǎnzé Xībānyá, tā juédìng dào **Nánměizhōu** de **Èguāduō'ěr** qù.

Amy has been learning Spanish since she was in secondary school, so when choosing a university to further improve her Spanish, Amy **decided** to be **bold**. She did not choose Spain; she decided to go to **Ecuador** in **South America**.

这次她去了一个很小的大学，这个大学在**安第斯山区**。在那一年里，她**接触**到了很多厄瓜多尔安第斯山区的**土著**孩子们，那一年给艾米**留下**了很多**美好**的**记忆**。

Zhècì tā qùle yígè hěn xiǎo de dàxué, zhège dàxué zài **Āndìsī shānqū**. Zài nà yì nián lǐ, tā **jiēchù** dàole hěnduō Èguāduō'ěr Āndìsī shānqū de **tǔzhù** háizimen, nà yì nián gěi Àimǐ **liú xià**le hěnduō **měihǎo** de **jìyì**.

This time she went to a small university in the **Andes**. During that year, she **came into contact with** many **Indigenous** children in the Ecuadorian Andes, and that year **left** Amy with many **wonderful memories**.

值得一提的是：艾米大三的时候，学院告诉学生们，他们如果想学中文，可以到中国的**天津外国语大学**学习一年。艾米知道这个机会很**难得**。

Zhídé yì tí de shì: Àimǐ dà sān de shíhou, xuéyuàn gàosù xuéshēngmen, tāmen rúguǒ xiǎng xué Zhōngwén, kěyǐ dào Zhōngguó de **Tiānjīn Wàiguóyǔ Dàxué** xuéxí yì nián. Àimǐ zhīdào **zhège** jīhuì hěn **nándé**.

It is **worth mentioning** that in Amy's third year, the college told students that if they wanted to learn Chinese, they could study for a year **at Tianjin Foreign Studies University in China**. Amy knew this **opportunity** was **precious**.

近十年来，越来越多的人开始学习中文，所以艾米选择了这个机会。到了天津以后，艾米才知道中文有多难，而且中国的文化和西方文化的**差异**又很大，所以这一年对艾米来说太难了！

149

Jìn shí nián lái, yuè lái yuè duō de rén kāishǐ xuéxí Zhōngwén, suǒyǐ Àimǐ xuǎnzéle zhège jīhuì. Dàole Tiānjīn yǐhòu, Àimǐ cái zhīdào Zhōngwén yǒu duō nàn, érqiě Zhōngguó de wénhuà hé Xīfāng wénhuà de **chāyì** yòu hěn dà, suǒyǐ zhè yì nián duì Àimǐ lái shuō tài nánle!

In the past ten years, more and more people began to learn Chinese, so Amy took this opportunity. After arriving in Tianjin, Amy learned how difficult Chinese is, and Chinese culture is very **different** from Western culture, so this year was very challenging for Amy!

头三个月，艾米只会说几句中文，三个月以后，她可以自己买东西，可还是很难。艾米在天津一共住了九个月，直到最后的一两个月她才开始觉得中文不那么难了！

Tóu sān gè yuè, Àimǐ zhǐ huì shuō jǐ jù Zhōngwén, sān gè yuè yǐhòu, tā kěyǐ zìjǐ mǎi dōngxi, kě hái shì hěn nán. Àimǐ zài Tiānjīn yígòng zhùle jiǔ gè yuè, zhídào zuìhòu de yì liǎng gè yuè tā cái kāishǐ juéde Zhōngwén bú nàme nánle!

For the first three months, Amy could only speak a few words of Chinese. After three months, she could buy things by herself, but it was still difficult. Amy lived in Tianjin for nine months, and it wasn't until the last month or two that she began to feel that Chinese was not that difficult!

现在艾米常常回想起自己六年的大学生活，**说起来**六年是很长的时间，可是自己那六年的大学过得好快啊！

Xiànzài Àimǐ chángcháng huíxiǎng qǐ zìjǐ liù nián de dàxué shēnghuó, **shuō qǐlái** liù nián shì hěn cháng de shíjiān, kěshì zìjǐ nà liù nián de dàxué guò de hǎo kuài a!

Now Amy often thinks back to her six years of uni life. **Speaking of** six years, it is a long time, but her six years of uni went by so fast!

总结/Summary

十八岁那年苏格兰女孩艾米接到了思克莱德大学的录取通知书，她好激动！在大学里，艾米主修西班牙文和意大利文。她的课程一共是五年。她要选择到说西班牙文和意大利文的国家各实习一年。艾米选择了意大利的维罗纳大学。在那里艾米学到了很多教外语的技能，同时也大大地提高了她自己的意大利文。她决定到南美洲的厄瓜多尔去进一步提高她的西班牙文。大学期间，艾米还去了中国的天津外国语大学学习了一年。说起来六年是很长的时间，可是艾米那六年的大学过得好快啊！

Shíbā suì nà nián Sūgélán nǚhái Àimǐ jiē dàole Sīkèláidé Dàxué de lùqǔ tōngzhīshū, tā hǎo jīdòng! Zài dàxué lǐ, Àimǐ zhǔ xiū Xībānyáwén hé Yìdàlìwén. Tā de kèchéng yígòng shì wǔ nián. Tā yào xuǎnzé dào shuō Xībānyáwén hé Yìdàlìwén de guójiā gè shíxí yì nián. Àimǐ xuǎnzéle Yìdàlì de Wéiluónà Dàxué. Zài nàlǐ Àimǐ xué dàole hěnduō jiāo wàiyǔ de jìnéng, tóngshí yě dàdà de tígāole tā zìjǐ de Yìdàlìwén. Tā juédìng dào Nánměizhōu de Èguāduō'ěr qù jìn yí bù tígāo tā de Xībānyáwén. Dàxué qījiān, Àimǐ hái qùle Zhōngguó de Tiānjīn Wàiguóyǔ Dàxué xuéxíle yì nián. Shuō qǐlái liù nián shì hěn cháng de shíjiān, kěshì Àimǐ nà liù nián de dàxué guò dé hǎo kuài a!

At the age of 18, Amy, a Scottish girl, received an offer from the University of Strathclyde. She was so excited! At university, Amy majored in Spanish and Italian. Her studies were five years in total. She needed to do a one-year internship in a country where Spanish and Italian, respectively, were spoken. Amy chose the University of Verona in Italy. Over there Amy learned many skills in teaching foreign languages, while also greatly improving her own Italian. She decided to go to Ecuador in South America to further improve her Spanish. During University, Amy also went to China's Tianjin Foreign

Studies University to study for a year. Speaking of six years sounds like a long time, but Amy's six years of uni life went by so fast!

生词/Vocabulary List

- 时代 – shídài: era, period
- 黄金 – huángjīn: gold, golden
- 年华 – niánhuá: years
- 压力 – yālì: pressure
- 自由 – zìyóu: freedom
- 追求 – zhuīqiú: to pursue
- 梦想 – mèngxiǎng: dream
- 努力 – nǔlì: to work hard
- 苏格兰 – Sūgélán: Scotland
- 酷 – kù: cool
- 思克莱德 – Sīkèláidé: Strathclyde
- 录取通知书 – lùqǔ tōngzhīshū: admission letter, offer
- 激动 – jīdòng: excited
- 展现 – zhǎnxiàn: to show
- 天赋 – tiānfù: genius
- 模仿 – mófǎng : to imitate
- 口音 – kǒuyīn: accent
- 初中 – chūzhōng: secondary school
- 选择 – xuǎnzé: to choose
- 西班牙语 – Xībānyáyǔ: Spanish
- 如鱼得水 – rúyúdéshuǐ: like a fish in water (Chinese idiom); glad to be in one's proper surroundings
- 自然地 – zìrán de: naturally
- 主修 – zhǔ xiū: to major in
- 意大利文 – Yìdàlìwén: Italian
- 课程 – kèchéng: course
- 学士 – xuéshì: Bachelor
- 学位 – xuéwèi: degree
- 之所以 – zhī suǒyǐ: the reason why
- 毕业 – bìyè: to graduate
- 专业 – zhuānyè: specialty field of study
- 实习 – shíxí: to practice, to be an intern
- 维罗纳 – Wéiluónà: Verona
- 联合国 – Liánhéguó: United Nations
- 教科文组织 – Jiàokēwén Zǔzhī: Educational, Scientific and Cultural Organization
- 世界遗产 – shìjiè yíchǎn: World Heritage Site

- 中世纪 – zhōngshìjì: Middle Ages
- 广场 – guǎngchǎng: square
- 喷泉 – pēnquán: fountain
- 建筑 – jiànzhù: architecture
- 更不要提 – gèng búyào tí: not to mention
- 美食 – měishí: delicious food
- 初学者 – chū xué zhě: beginner
- 技能 – jìnéng: skill
- 决定 – juédìng: decide
- 大胆 – dàdǎn: bold
- 南美洲 – Nánměizhōu: South America
- 厄瓜多尔 – Èguāduō'ěr: Ecuador
- 安第斯山区 – Āndìsī shānqū: Andes
- 接触 – jiēchù: come into contact
- 土著 – tǔzhù: Indigenous
- 留下 – liú xià: to stay, to remain
- 美好 – měihǎo: happy, fine
- 记忆 – jìyì: memory
- 值得一提 – zhídé yì tí: worth mentioning
- 天津外国语大学 – Tiānjīn Wàiguóyǔ Dàxué: Tianjin Foreign Studies University
- 机会 – jīhuì: opportunity
- 难得 – nándé: rare
- 差异 – chāyì: difference
- 说起来 – shuō qǐlái: speaking of

问题/Questions

1. 上初中的时候，艾米觉得西班牙文很难。

   At secondary school, Amy found Spanish difficult.

   A. 对
   B. 错

2. 艾米选择了苏格兰的爱丁堡大学。

   Amy chose Edinburgh University in Scotland.

   A. 对
   B. 错

3. 下面的哪门语言艾米不会说？

   Which of the following languages does Amy not speak?

   A. 西班牙文
   B. 意大利文
   C. 日文
   D. 英文

4. 艾米去了中国的哪个大学？

   Which university in China did Amy go to?

   A. 厦门大学
   B. 上海复旦大学
   C. 北京大学
   D. 天津外国语大学

5. 艾米觉得中文不太难。

   Amy thinks Chinese is not too difficult.

   A. 对
   B. 错

答案/Answers

1. B 错
   False

2. B 错
   False

3. C 日文
   Japanese

4. D 天津外国语大学
   Tianjin Foreign Studies University

5. B 错
   False

CHAPTER 13

退休生活 – RETIREMENT LIFE

洛琳在伦敦的**金融业**工作三十多年了。这三十多年里，她**换**了很多工作，大多数的工作她都很喜欢。女儿也长大了，今年二十五岁了！洛琳对自己说再过五年就好了，就到了**法定**的退休**年龄**了。

洛琳年轻的时候很喜欢艺术，她想过要当**艺术家**，可是现实的生活让她**放弃**了那个**愿望**。女儿在**私立**学校上学，每年的**学费**很贵。洛琳的房子也有**贷款**，每个月的**按揭**需要丈夫和洛琳两个人**负担**，一转眼二三十年就过去了。有时候洛琳会做**白日梦**，**梦想**自己是一个艺术家。

今年**圣诞节**假期的时候，洛琳又和丈夫说起了自己年轻时候的梦想，洛琳希望退休后可以学**摄影**、画**油画**、写**个人博客**。丈夫看了看**满眼**都是**期待**的洛琳，问她为什么要等到退休以后呢？为什么不现在就开始呢？洛琳从没想过自己有**提前**退休的选择。她丈夫说房子的贷款已经还完了，女儿也长大了，如果洛琳打算学摄影、画油画、写个人博客，那么她今年就可以开始做这些事情。

两个月以后，洛琳**辞职**了，开始了她的退休生活。她每天早上上摄影课，下午上艺术课，晚上在**电脑**上写她的博客，非常地忙，都没有时间做**家务**。丈夫有时候**开玩笑**说自己建议洛琳早退休不是一个好主意，现在在家里他比以前做家务做得多多了！

洛琳现在每天的生活都很**充实**，她比上班的时候忙多了！可是她每天都很快乐，每天都在学习做新的和自己**喜爱**的东西。

退休生活– Retirement Life
With English Translation

洛琳在伦敦的**金融业**工作三十多年了。这三十多年里，她**换**了很多工作，大多数的工作她都很喜欢。女儿也长大了，今年二十五岁了！

Luòlín zài Lúndūn de **jīnróng yè** gōngzuò sānshí duō nián le. Zhè sānshí duō nián lǐ, tā **huàn**le hěnduō gōngzuò, dàduōshù de gōngzuò tā dōu hěn xǐhuān. Nǚ'ér yě zhǎng dàle, jīnnián èrshíwǔ suì le!

Lorraine has worked in the **financial industry** in London for over thirty years. In the past 30 years, she has **changed** to many different jobs, most of which she liked very much. Her daughter has also grown up now and is twenty-five years old this year!

洛琳对自己说再过五年就好了，就到了**法定**的退休**年龄**了。

Luòlín duì zìjǐ shuō zài guò wǔ nián jiù hǎole, jiù dàole **fǎdìng** de tuìxiū **niánlíng** le.

Lorraine said to herself that it would be good in five years' time when she had reached the **legal** retirement **age**.

洛琳年轻的时候很喜欢艺术，她想过要当**艺术家**，可是现实的生活让她**放弃**了那个**愿望**。女儿在**私立**学校上学，每年的**学费**很贵。

Luòlín niánqīng de shíhou hěn xǐhuān yìshù, tā xiǎng guò yào dāng **yìshùjiā**, kěshì xiànshí de shēnghuó ràng tā **fàngqì**le nàgè **yuànwàng**. Nǚ'ér zài **sīlì** xuéxiào shàngxué, měinián de **xuéfèi** hěn guì.

Lorraine liked art very much when she was young. She wanted to be an **artist**, but real life made her **give up** that **wish**. Her daughter went to a **private** school, and the annual **school fee** was very expensive.

洛琳的房子也有**贷款**，每个月的**按揭**需要丈夫和洛琳两个人**负担**，一转眼二三十年就过去了。有时候洛琳会做**白日梦**，梦想自己是一个艺术家。

Luòlín de fángzi yěyǒu **dàikuǎn**, měi gè yuè de **ànjiē** xūyào zhàngfū hé Luòlín liǎng gè rén **fùdān**, **yì zhuǎn yǎn** èrsānshí nián jiù guòqùle. Yǒu shíhou Luólán huì zuò **báirìmèng**, mèngxiǎng zìjǐ shì yígè yìshùjiā.

Lorraine's house also had a **mortgage**, and the monthly **payment** needed to be **borne** by her husband and Lorraine. Thirty years have passed by **in a blink of an eye**. Sometimes Lorraine would **daydream** about being an artist.

今年**圣诞节**假期的时候，洛琳又和丈夫说起了自己年轻时候的梦想，洛琳希望退休后可以学**摄影**、画**油画**、写**个人博客**。

Jīnnián **Shèngdànjié** jiàqī de shíhou, Luòlín yòu hé zhàngfū shuō qǐle zìjǐ niánqīng shíhou de mèngxiǎng, Luòlín xīwàng tuìxiū hòu kěyǐ xué **shèyǐng**, huà **yóuhuà**, xiě **gèrén bókè**.

During the **Christmas** holiday this year, Lorraine talked to her husband about the dream she had when she was young. Lorraine said she hoped to learn **photography**, do **oil paintings**, and write a **personal blog** after retirement.

丈夫看了看**满眼**都是**期待**的洛琳，问她为什么要等到退休以后呢？为什么不现在就开始呢？洛琳从没想过自己有**提前**退休的选择。

Zhàngfū kànle kàn **mǎn yǎn** dōu shì **qīdài** de Luòlín, wèn tā wèishénme yào děng dào tuìxiū yǐhòu ne? Wèishénme bù xiànzài jiù kāishǐ ne? Luò líncóng méi xiǎng guò zìjǐ yǒu **tíqián** tuìxiū de xuǎnzé.

Her husband looked at Lorraine, whose eyes were **full of anticipation**, and asked her why she had to wait until after retirement? Why not start now? Lorraine never thought she had the option to retire **early**.

她丈夫说房子的贷款已经还完了，女儿也长大了，如果洛琳打算学摄影、画油画、写个人博客，那么她今年就可以开始做这些事情。

Tā zhàngfū shuō fángzi de dàikuǎn yǐjīng huán wánle, nǚ'ér yě zhǎngdàle, rúguǒ Luòlín dǎsuàn xué shèyǐng, huà yóuhuà, xiě gèrén bókè, nàme tā jīnnián jiù kěyǐ kāishǐ zuò zhèxiē shìqing.

Her husband said that the mortgage on their house had been paid off, and their daughter had grown up. If Lorraine planned to learn photography, do oil paintings and write a personal blog, she could start doing those things this year.

两个月以后，洛琳**辞职**了，开始了她的退休生活。她每天早上上摄影课，下午上艺术课，晚上在**电脑**上写她的博客，非常地忙，都没有时间做**家务**。

Liǎng gè yuè yǐhòu, Luòlín **cízhí**le, kāishǐle tā de tuìxiū shēnghuó. Tā měitiān zǎoshang shàng shèyǐng kè, xiàwǔ shàng yìshù kè, wǎnshang zài **diànnǎo** shàng xiě tā de bókè, fēicháng de máng, dōu méiyǒu shíjiān zuò **jiāwù**.

Two months later, Lorraine **resigned** and began her retirement life. She takes photography class in the morning, art class in the afternoon, and writes her blog on the **computer** in the evening. She is so busy that she has no time to do **housework**.

丈夫有时候**开玩笑**说自己建议洛琳早退休不是一个好主意，现在在家里他比以前做家务做得多多了！

Zhàngfū yǒu shíhou **kāiwánxiào** shuō zìjǐ jiànyì Luòlín zǎo tuìxiū búshì yígè hǎo zhǔyì, xiànzài zài jiālǐ tā bǐ yǐqián zuò jiāwù zuò de duō duōle!

Her husband sometimes **jokes** that it was not a good idea to suggest Lorraine retire early, and now he is doing more housework at home than before!

洛琳现在每天的生活都很**充实**，她比上班的时候忙多了！可是她每天都很快乐，每天都在学习做新的和自己**喜爱的东西**。

Luòlín xiànzài měitiān de shēnghuó dōu hěn **chōngshí**, tā bǐ shàngbān de shíhou máng duōle! Kěshì tā měitiān dōu hěn kuàilè, měitiān dōu zài xuéxí zuò xīn de hé zìjǐ **xǐ'ài de dōngxi**.

Now Lorraine's life is very **fulfilling** every day; she is much busier than when she was at work! But she is happy every day, learning to do something new and **something** she **loves** every day.

总结/Summary

洛琳在伦敦的金融业工作三十多年了。再过五年她就到了法定的退休年龄了。洛琳年轻的时候想过要当艺术家，可是现实的生活让她放弃了那个愿望。今年圣诞节假期的时候，洛琳又和丈夫说起了自己年轻时候的梦想，洛琳希望退休后可以学摄影、画油画、写个人博客。丈夫问她为什么要等到退休以后呢？两个月以后，洛琳辞职了，开始了她的退休生活。现在她比上班的时候忙多了，都没有时间做家务了！可是她每天都很快乐，每天都在学习做新的和自己喜爱的东西。

Luòlín zài Lúndūn de jīnróng yè gōngzuò sānshí duō niánle. Zài guò wǔ nián tā jiù dàole fǎdìng de tuìxiū niánlíng le. Luòlín niánqīng de shíhou xiǎng guò yào dāng yìshùjiā, kěshì xiànshí de shēnghuó ràng tā fàngqìle nàgè yuànwàng. Jīnnián Shèngdànjié jiàqī de shíhou, Luòlín yòu hé zhàngfū shuō qǐle zìjǐ niánqīng shíhou de mèngxiǎng, Luòlín xīwàng tuìxiū hòu kěyǐ xué shèyǐng, huà yóuhuà, xiě gèrén bókè. Zhàngfū wèn tā wèishénme yào děng dào tuìxiū yǐhòu ne? Liǎng gè yuè yǐhòu, Luòlín cízhíle, kāishǐle tā de tuìxiū shēnghuó. Xiànzài tā bǐ shàngbān de shíhou máng duō le, dōu méiyǒu shíjiān zuò jiāwùle! Kěshì tā měitiān dōu hěn kuàilè, měitiān dōu zài xuéxí zuò xīn de hé zìjǐ xǐ'ài de dōngxi.

Lorraine has worked in the financial industry in London for over thirty years. In five years, she will reach the legal retirement age. Lorraine wanted to be an artist when she was young, but reality made her give up that wish. During the Christmas holiday this year, Lorraine talked to her husband about her dream she had when she was young. Lorraine hoped to learn photography, paint oil paintings, and write a personal blog after retirement. Her husband asked her why she had to wait until after retirement? Two months later, Lorraine resigned and began her retirement life. Now she is much busier than when she was at work, and she has no time to do housework! But she is happy, learning to do something new and something she loves every day.

生词/Vocabulary List

- 金融业 – jīnróng yè: financial industry
- 换 – huàn: to exchange
- 法定 – fǎdìng: legal
- 年龄 – niánlíng: age
- 艺术家 – yìshùjiā: artist
- 放弃 – fàngqì: to give up
- 愿望 – yuànwàng : desire
- 私立 – sīlì: private
- 学费 – xuéfèi: tuition fee
- 贷款 – dàikuǎn: mortgage, loan
- 按揭 – ànjiē: mortgage payment
- 负担 – fùdān: to bear a burden, burden
- 一转眼 – yì zhuǎn yǎn: a blink of an eye
- 白日梦 – báirìmèng: daydream
- 梦想 – mèngxiǎng: dream
- 圣诞节 – Shèngdànjié: Christmas
- 摄影 – shèyǐng: photography
- 油画 – yóuhuà: oil painting
- 个人博客 – gèrén bókè: personal blog
- 满 – mǎn: full, filled
- 期待 – qīdài: to anticipate, anticipation
- 辞职 – cízhí: to resign
- 电脑 – diànnǎo: computer
- 家务 – jiāwù: housework
- 开玩笑 - kāiwánxiào: to make a joke
- 充实 – chōngshí: fulfilling
- 喜爱 – xǐ'ài : to love, to like, favorite
- 东西 – dōngxi: things

问题/Questions

1. 洛琳有一个儿子，他今年二十五岁。

   Lorraine has a son who is twenty-five years old this year.

   A. 对
   B. 错

2. 再过十年，洛琳就到了法定的退休年龄了。

   Lorraine will reach the legal retirement age in ten years.

   A. 对
   B. 错

3. 洛琳年轻的时候想当作家。

   Lorraine wanted to be a writer when she was young.

   A. 对
   B. 错

4. 退休以后，洛琳不想做什么？

   What does Lorraine not want to do after retirement?

   A. 学摄影
   B. 画油画
   C. 写个人博客
   D. 写小说

5. 辞职以后，洛琳有更多的时间做家务？

   Lorraine has more time to do housework after quitting her job.

   A. 对
   B. 错

答案/Answers

1. B 错
   False

2. B 错
   False

3. B 错
   False

4. D 写小说
   Write novels

5. B 错
   False

CHAPTER 14

工作与生活的平衡 –
WORK AND LIFE BALANCE

我们生活在一个**信息爆炸**的时代。现在的信息每七年到十年就**翻一番**，我们每个人都在不停地学习新的信息，**要不然就会被社会淘汰**。

贝佳娜就很有**感触**。她今年三十岁，已经在英国的巴克莱银行工作六年了。她是一个**数据分析师**，整天跟数据**打交道**。在工作中，她要不停地学习新的数据**编程语言**，她的生活只有她的工作。每周一到周五，她大概要工作五十个小时。周末的时候，她要做家务、**购物**和休息，很少有时间去看朋友和家人。

两年以前，有一段时间她的工作压力很大，**同事**间不**友好**，有很多人际关系的矛盾。几个月的时间，她**掉**了五公斤，**身心疲惫**！

经过了那几个月，她**意识**到工作与生活的**平衡**很重要。工作是生活的一**部分**，不是生活的**全部**。她下决心要**改变**她的生活，决定从**调整**她的饮食开始。

她以前总是在外面买饭，自己很少做饭。现在她尽量自己做饭，少吃**加工过**的**食品**，主要吃**新鲜**的**有机**食品。每个星期她还**挤出**时间去两次**健身房**。两个月以后，她的**皮肤**好多了，**脑子**也快了，她还注意到她的**精神**也好多了。

167

半年以后，她开始**练瑜伽功**，她发现瑜伽功让她感觉放松了很多，她的**睡眠质量**也提高了。现在在工作中，如果她有压力，她都会**提醒**自己做**深呼吸**，让自己放松下来。

工作与生活的平衡– Work and Life Balance
With English Translation

我们生活在一个**信息爆炸**的时代。现在的信息每七年到十年就**翻一番**，我们每个人都在不停地学习新的信息，**要不然就会被社会淘汰**。

Wǒmen shēnghuó zài yígè xìnxī **bàozhà** de shídài. Xiànzài de xìnxī měi qī nián dào shí nián jiù **fān yì fān**, wǒmen měi gè rén dōu zài bù tíng de xuéxí xīn de xìnxī, **yào bù rán** jiù huì **bèi shèhuì táotài.**

We live in an era of **information explosion.** The amount of available information is now **doubling** every seven to ten years, and every one of us is constantly learning new information, **otherwise we will be made redundant by society**.

贝佳娜就很有**感触**。她今年三十岁，已经在英国的巴克莱银行工作六年了。她是一个**数据分析师**，整天跟数据**打交道**。在工作中，她要不停地学习新的数据**编程语言**，她的生活只有她的工作。

Bèijiānà jiù hěn yǒu **gǎnchù**. Tā jīnnián sānshí suì, yǐjīng zài Yīngguó de Bākèlái Yínháng gōngzuò liù nián le. Tā shì yígè **shùjù fēnxīshī**, zhěng tiān gēn shùjù **dǎjiāodào**. Zài gōngzuò zhōng, tā yào bù tíng de xuéxí xīn de shùjù **biānchéng yǔyán**, tā de shēnghuó zhǐyǒu tā de gōngzuò.

Bejana is **feeling** it. She is 30 years old and has been with Barclays Bank in the UK for six years. She is a **data analyst** and **works with** data all day. At work, she is constantly learning new data **programming languages**, and her life is nothing but her work.

每周一到周五，她大概要工作五十个小时。周末的时候，她要做家务、**购物**和休息，很少有时间去看朋友和家人。

Měi zhōuyī dào zhōuwǔ, tā dàgài yào gōngzuò wǔshí gè xiǎoshí. Zhōumò de shíhou, tā yào zuò jiāwù, **gòuwù** hé xiūxi, hěn shǎo yǒu shíjiān qù kàn péngyǒu hé jiārén

She works about fifty hours a week from Monday to Friday. On weekends, she does housework, **shopping** and she rests, and rarely has time to see friends and family.

两年以前，有一段时间她的工作压力很大，**同事**间不**友好**，有很多人际关系的矛盾。几个月的时间，她**掉**了五公斤，**身心疲惫**！

Liǎng nián yǐqián, yǒu yíduàn shíjiān tā de gōngzuò yālì hěn dà, **tóngshì** jiān bù **yǒuhǎo**, yǒu hěnduō **rénjì guānxì** de **máodùn**. Jǐ gè yuè de shíjiān, tā **diào**le wǔ gōngjīn, **shēnxīn píbèi**!

Two years ago, there was a time when she had lots of pressure at work, her **colleagues** were **unfriendly**, and there were many **interpersonal relationship conflicts**. In a few months, she **lost** five kilograms and was **physically and mentally exhausted**!

经过了那几个月，她**意识**到工作与生活的**平衡**很重要。工作是生活的一**部分**，不是生活的**全部**。她下决心要**改变**她的生活，决定从**调整**她的饮食开始。

Jīngguòle nà jǐ gè yuè, tā **yìshí** dào gōngzuò yǔ shēnghuó de **pínghéng** hěn zhòngyào. Gōngzuò shì shēnghuó de **yíbùfēn**, búshì shēnghuó de **quánbù**. Tā xià juéxīn yào **gǎibiàn** tā de shēnghuó, juédìng cóng **tiáozhěng** tā de yǐnshí kāishǐ.

After these few months, she **realized** that work-life **balance** is important. Work is **part** of life, rather than the **whole** of life. She was determined to **change** her situation and decided to start by **adjusting** her diet.

她以前总是在外面买饭，自己很少做饭。现在她尽量自己做饭，少吃**加工过**的**食品**，主要吃**新鲜**的**有机**食品。

Tā yǐqián zǒngshì zài wàimiàn mǎi fàn, zìjǐ hěn shǎo zuò fàn. Xiànzài tā jǐnliàng zìjǐ zuò fàn, shǎo chī **jiāgōngguò** de **shípǐn**, zhǔyào chī **xīnxiān** de **yǒujī** shípǐn.

She used to always eat out and rarely cook herself. Now she cooks as much as she can and eats less **processed food** and mostly eats **fresh organic** food.

每个星期她还**挤**出时间去两次**健身房**。两个月以后，她的**皮肤**好多了，**脑子**也快了，她还注意到她的**精神**也好多了.

Měi gè xīngqī tā hái **jǐ** chū shíjiān qù liǎng cì **jiànshēnfáng**. Liǎng gè yuè yǐhòu, tā de **pífū** hǎoduōle, **nǎozi** yě kuàile, tā hái zhùyì dào tā de **jīngshén** yě hǎoduōle.

She also **finds** time to go to the **gym** twice a week. Two months later, her **skin** is much better, **her brain** is faster, and she also noticed that she is in better spirits.

半年以后，她开始练**瑜伽功**，她发现瑜伽功让她感觉放松了很多，她的**睡眠质量**也提高了。现在在工作中，如果她有压力，她都会**提醒**自己做**深呼吸**，让自己放松下来。

Bànnián yǐhòu, tā kāishǐ liàn **yújiā gōng**, tā fāxiàn yújiā gōng ràng tā gǎnjué fàngsōngle hěnduō, tā de **shuìmián zhìliàng** yě tígāole. Xiànzài zài gōngzuò zhōng, rúguǒ tā yǒu yālì, tā dōu huì **tíxǐng** zìjǐ zuò **shēnhūxī**, ràng zìjǐ fàngsōng xiàlái.

Half a year later, she started **practicing yoga**, and she found that yoga made her feel more relaxed and her **sleep quality** improved. Now at work, if she is stressed, she **reminds** herself to **take deep breaths** and relax.

总结/Summary

贝佳娜今年三十岁，已经在英国的巴克莱银行工作六年了。在工作中，她要不停地学习新的数据编程语言，她的生活只有她的工作。两年以前，有一段时间她的工作压力很大，同事间不友好。几个月的时间，她掉了五公斤，身心疲惫！经过了那几个月，她意识到工作与生活的平衡很重要。她下决心要改变她的生活，决定从调整她的饮食开始。每个星期她还挤出时间去两次健身房。半年以后，她开始练瑜伽功，她发现瑜伽功让她感觉放松了很多，她的睡眠质量也提高了。

Bèijiānà jīnnián sānshí suì, yǐjīng zài Yīngguó de Bākèlái Yínháng gōngzuò liù nián le. Zài gōngzuò zhōng, tā yào bù tíng de xuéxí xīn de shùjù biānchéng yǔyán, tā de shēnghuó zhǐyǒu tā de gōngzuò. Liǎng nián yǐqián, yǒu yíduàn shíjiān tā de gōngzuò yālì hěn dà, tóngshì jiān bù yǒuhǎo. Jǐ gè yuè de shíjiān, tā diàole wǔ gōngjīn, shēnxīn píbèi! Jīngguòle nà jǐ gè yuè, tā yìshí dào gōngzuò yǔ shēnghuó de pínghéng hěn zhòngyào. Tā xià juéxīn yào gǎibiàn tā de shēnghuó, juédìng cóng tiáozhěng tā de yǐnshí kāishǐ. Měi gè xīngqī tā hái jǐ chū shíjiān qù liǎng cì jiànshēnfáng. Bànnián yǐhòu, tā kāishǐ liàn yújiā gōng, tā fāxiàn yújiā gōng ràng tā gǎnjué fàngsōngle hěnduō, tā de shuìmián zhìliàng yě tígāole.

Bejana, who is thirty years old, has been with Barclays in the UK for six years. At work, she is constantly learning new data programming languages, and her life was nothing but her work. Two years ago, there was a time when her job was stressful, and her colleagues were unfriendly. She lost five kilograms in a few months and was physically and mentally exhausted! After those few months, she realized that work-life balance is important. Determined to change her life, she decided to start by adjusting her diet. She also found time to go to the gym twice a week. She started practicing yoga half a year later, and she found that yoga made her feel more relaxed, and her sleep quality improved as well.

生词/Vocabulary List

- 信息 – xìnxī: information
- 爆炸 – bàozhà: to explode, explosion
- 翻一番 – fān yì fān: to double
- 要不然 – yào bù rán: otherwise
- 被 – bèi: passive marker
- 社会 – shèhuì: society
- 淘汰 – táotài: to be made redundant
- 感触 – gǎnchù: to feel
- 数据 – shùjù: data
- 分析师 – fēnxīshī: analyst
- 打交道 – dǎjiāodào: to deal with
- 编程语言 – biānchéng yǔyán: programming language
- 购物 – gòuwù: shopping
- 同事 – tóngshì: colleague
- 不友好 – bù yǒuhǎo: unfriendly
- 人际关系 – rénjì guānxì: interpersonal relationship
- 矛盾 – máodùn: conflict
- 掉 – diào: to lose

- 身心疲惫 – shēnxīn píbèi: to be exhausted
- 意识 – yìshí: to realize
- 平衡 – pínghéng: balance
- 部分 – bùfēn: part
- 全部 – quánbù: all
- 改变 – gǎibiàn: change, to change
- 调整 – tiáozhěng: to adjust, adjustment
- 加工过 – jiāgōngguò: processed
- 食品 – shípǐn: food
- 新鲜 – xīnxiān: fresh
- 有机 – yǒujī: organic
- 挤 – jǐ: to squeeze
- 健身房 – jiànshēnfáng: gym
- 皮肤 – pífū: skin
- 脑子 – nǎozi: brain
- 精神 – jīngshén: spirits
- 练 – liàn: to practice
- 瑜伽功 – yújiā gōng: yoga
- 睡眠质量 – shuìmián zhìliàng: sleep quality
- 提醒 – tíxǐng: to remind
- 深呼吸 – shēnhūxī: to take a deep breath

174

问题/Questions

1. 贝佳娜在一家美国银行工作六年了。

   Bejana has worked for a US bank for six years.

   A. 对
   B. 错

2. 周一到周五，贝佳娜工作四十个小时。

   Bejana worked forty hours from Monday to Friday.

   A. 对
   B. 错

3. 两年以前，在贝佳娜的工作中下面哪件事情没有发生？

   Which of the following did not happen at Bejana's job two years ago?

   A. 压力很大
   B. 人际关系的矛盾
   C. 同事间不友好
   D. 她升职了

4. 贝佳娜意识到工作与生活的平衡很重要。

   Bejana realizes that a work-life balance is important.

   A. 对
   B. 错

5. 贝佳娜挤出时间每个星期去两次健身房。

   Bejana found time to go to the gym twice a week.

   A. 对
   B. 错

答案/Answers

1. B 错
   False

2. B 错
   False

3. D 她升职了
   She got promoted

4. A 对
   True

5. A 对
   True

CHAPTER 15

学外语有最佳年龄吗？–
IS THERE AN OPTIMAL AGE TO LEARN A FOREIGN LANGUAGE?

大家都说学语言是越早越好，小的时候**模仿能力强**，学外语很快。我**同意**！今天我们来**聊聊劳拉**学习外语的**经历**。

劳拉今年五十九岁了，她是美国纽约人。直到六七年前，她都是小学老师。五十岁的时候，她决定从学校**辞职**去**亚洲**旅游和**生活**。两个女儿都长大了。她的房子贷款也还完了。她想**换**一种生活**方式**。

到亚洲哪里呢？做什么呢？劳拉以前去过马来西亚，她很喜欢那里。朋友建议她教英语。她觉得这个主意很好。很容易地她就找到了一份英语老师的工作。她的工作很**灵活**，而且她的假期也很多。四五年的时间，她去了亚洲很多的国家和地区，**体验**了很多新的文化。没有想到的是：她**迷**上了中文和马来文。她去中国**云南**的语言学校学习了两个月。**新冠肺炎**期间，她不得不回美国居住，在美国的两年她一直**坚持**学习中文，**时时刻刻**都不**放松**。她参加了很多中文**口语**练习班。今年五月她还考过了**汉语水平四级考试**。她不敢相信自己**居然**通过了。她的马来文现在也很好，用马来文和朋友聊天一点儿问题也没有。

她的中文和马来文**口音**都很**标准**。我同意很多东西都是小时候比较容易学，可是年纪大一点的时候也不是不能学。只要你想学，**不怕下功夫**，什么年纪都可以学好外语。

学外语有最佳年龄吗？– Is There an Optimal Age to Learn a Foreign Language?
With English Translation

大家都说学语言是越早越好，小的时候**模仿能力强**，学外语很快。我**同意**！今天我们来**聊聊劳拉**学习外语的**经历**。

Dàjiā dōu shuō xué yǔyán shì yuè zǎo yuè hǎo, xiǎo de shíhou mófǎng nénglì qiáng, xué wàiyǔ hěn kuài. Wǒ **tóngyì**! Jīntiān wǒmen lái **liáo liáo Láolā** xuéxí wàiyǔ de **jīnglì**.

Everyone says that the younger you start to learn a language, the better it is. When you are young, you have a strong **ability** to **imitate** and learn foreign languages quickly. **I agree**! Today we are going to **chat about Laura**'s **experience** of learning a foreign language.

劳拉今年五十九岁了，她是美国纽约人。直到六七年前，她都是小学老师。

Láolā jīnnián wǔshíjiǔ suì le, tā shì Měiguó Niǔyuē rén. Zhídào liù qī nián qián, tā dōu shì xiǎoxué lǎoshī.

Laura is fifty-nine years old this year. She is from New York, USA. She was a primary school teacher until six or seven years ago.

五十岁的时候，她决定从学校**辞职**去**亚洲**旅游和**生活**。两个女儿都长大了。她的房子贷款也还完了。她想**换**一种生活**方式**。

Wǔshí suì de shíhou, tā juédìng cóng xuéxiào **cízhí** qù **Yàzhōu** lǚyóu hé **shēnghuó**. Liǎng gè nǚ'ér dōu zhǎng dàle. Tā de fángzi dàikuǎn yě huán wánle. Tā xiǎng **huàn** yì zhǒng shēnghuó **fāngshì**.

At the age of fifty, she decided to **quit** teaching school to travel and **live** in **Asia**. Both her daughters have grown up. The mortgage on the house has also been paid off. She wants to **change** her life**style**.

178

到亚洲哪里呢？做什么呢？劳拉以前去过马来西亚，她很喜欢那里。朋友建议她教英语。她觉得这个主意很好。

Dào Yàzhōu nǎlǐ ne? Zuò shénme ne? Láolā yǐqián qùguò Mǎláixīyà, tā hěn xǐhuān nàlǐ. Péngyǒu jiànyì tā jiāo Yīngyǔ. Tā juéde zhège zhǔyì hěn hǎo.

Where to go in Asia? What to do? Laura had been to Malaysia before, and she loved it. Friends suggested she could teach English. She thought that was a good idea.

很容易地她就找到了一份英语老师的工作。她的工作很**灵活**，而且她的假期也很多。四五年的时间，她去了亚洲很多的国家和地区，**体验**了很多新的文化。

Hěn róngyì de tā jiù zhǎodàole yí fèn Yīngyǔ lǎoshī de gōngzuò. Tā de gōngzuò hěn **línghuó**, érqiě tā de jiàqī yě hěnduō. Sìwǔ nián de shíjiān, tā qùle Yàzhōu hěnduō de guójiā hé dìqū, **tǐyàn**le hěnduō xīn de wénhuà.

She found a job as an English teacher easily. Her work is **flexible**, and she also has a lot of holidays. Within four to five years, she went to many countries and regions in Asia and **experienced** many new cultures.

没有想到的是：她迷上了中文和马来文。她去中国**云南**的语言学校学习了两个月。**新冠肺炎**期间，她不得不回美国居住，在美国的两年她一直**坚持**学习中文，**时时刻刻**都不**放松**。

Méiyǒu xiǎng dào de shì: Tā **mí shàng**le Zhōngwén hé Mǎláiwén. Tā qù Zhōngguó **Yúnnán** de yǔyán xuéxiào xuéxíle liǎng gè yuè. **Xīnguān fèiyán** qíjiān, tā bù dé bù huí měiguó jūzhù, zài měiguó de liǎng nián tā yìzhí **jiānchí** xuéxí Zhōngwén, **shí shí kè kè** dōu bú **fàngsōng**.

She became **obsessed** with Chinese and Malay unexpectedly. She went to a language school in **Yunnan**, China, to study for two months.

179

During **COVID-19**, she had to return to the US to live. During the two years in the US, she **remained committed to** learning Chinese and never **relaxed.**

她参加了很多中文口语练习班。今年五月她还考过了汉语水平四级考试。她不敢相信自己居然通过了。她的马来文现在也很好，用马来文和朋友聊天一点儿问题也没有。

Tā cānjiāle hěnduō Zhōngwén **kǒuyǔ** liànxí bān. Jīnnián wǔ yuè tā hái kǎo guòle Hànyǔ **Shuǐpíng Sìjí Kǎoshì**. Tā bù gǎn xiāngxìn zìjǐ **jūrán** tōngguòle. Tā de Mǎláiwén xiànzài yě hěn hǎo, yòng Mǎláiwén hé péngyǒu liáotiān yìdiǎnr wèntí yě méiyǒu.

She attended many Chinese **speaking** practice classes. She also passed **Hanyu Shuiping Kaoshi (Level 4)** in May, this year. She couldn't believe she **passed** it. Her Malay is also very good now and she has no problem at all chatting with friends in Malay.

她的中文和马来文口音都很标准。我同意很多东西都是小时候比较容易学，可是年纪大一点的时候也不是不能学。

Tā de Zhōngwén hé Mǎláiwén **kǒuyīn** dōu hěn **biāozhǔn**. Wǒ tóngyì hěnduō dōngxi dōu shì xiǎoshíhou bǐjiào róngyì xué, kěshì niánjì dà yìdiǎn de shíhou yě búshì bùnéng xué.

Both her Chinese and Malay **accents** are very **authentic**. I agree that many things are easier to learn when you are young, but it is not impossible to learn when you are older too.

只要你想学，不怕下功夫，什么年纪都可以学好外语。

Zhǐyào nǐ xiǎng xué, búpà **xià gōngfu**, **shénme niánjì** dōu kěyǐ xué hǎo wàiyǔ.

You can learn foreign languages well **at any age** as long as you want to learn and are not **afraid to put in the effort.**

总结/Summary

劳拉今年五十九岁了，她是美国纽约人。五十岁的时候，她决定从学校辞职去亚洲旅游和生活。她想换一种生活方式。她在马来西亚找到了一份英语老师的工作。四五年的时间，她去了亚洲很多的国家和地区，体验了很多新的文化。没有想到的是：她迷上了中文和马来文。今年五月她还考过了汉语水平四级考试。她的马来文现在也很好，用马来文和朋友聊天一点儿问题也没有。只要你想学，不怕下功夫，什么年纪都可以学好外语。

Láolā jīnnián wǔshíjiǔ suì le, tā shì Měiguó Niǔyuē rén. Wǔshí suì de shíhou, tā juédìng cóng xuéxiào cízhí qù Yàzhōu lǚyóu hé shēnghuó. Tā xiǎng huàn yì zhǒng shēnghuó fāngshì. Tā zài Mǎláixīyà zhǎodàole yífèn Yīngyǔ lǎoshī de gōngzuò. Sì wǔ nián de shíjiān, tā qùle Yàzhōu hěnduō de guójiā hé dìqū, tǐyànle hěnduō xīn de wénhuà. Méiyǒu xiǎngdào de shì: Tā mí shàngle Zhōngwén hé Mǎláiwén. Jīnnián wǔ yuè tā hái kǎoguòle Hànyǔ Shuǐpíng Sìjí Kǎoshì. Tā de Mǎláiwén xiànzài yě hěn hǎo, yòng Mǎláiwén hé péngyǒu liáotiān yìdiǎnr wèntí yě méiyǒu. Zhǐyào nǐ xiǎng xué, búpà xià gōngfu, shénme niánjì dōu kěyǐ xuéhǎo wàiyǔ.

Laura is fifty-nine years old. She is from New York, USA. At the age of fifty, she decided to quit her job at school to travel and live in Asia. She wanted to change her way of life. She got a job as an English teacher in Malaysia. She went to many countries and regions in Asia and experienced many new cultures within four to five years. She unexpectedly became obsessed with Chinese and Malay. She also passed Hanyu Shuiping Kaoshi (Level 4) in May this year. Her Malay is also very good now. She has no problem chatting with friends in Malay at all. As long as you want to learn and are not afraid to put in the effort, you can learn foreign languages well at any age.

生词/Vocabulary List

- 模仿 – mófǎng: to imitate
- 能力 – nénglì: ability
- 强 – qiáng: better, powerful
- 同意 – tóngyì: to agree
- 聊聊 – liáo liáo: to chat
- 辞职 – cízhí: to quit, to resign
- 亚洲 – Yàzhōu: Asia
- 生活 – shēnghuó: life, living
- 换 – huàn: to change
- 方式 – fāngshì: style
- 灵活 – línghuó: flexible
- 体验 – tǐyàn: to experience, experience
- 迷上 – mí shàng: hooked
- 新冠肺炎 – xīnguān fèiyán: COVID-19
- 坚持 – jiānchí: to remain committed to, stick to
- 时时刻刻 – shí shí kè kè: all the time
- 放松 – fàngsōng: to relax
- 口语 – kǒuyǔ: spoken language
- 汉语水平四级考试 – Hànyǔ Shuǐpíng Sìjí Kǎoshì: HSK level 4, Chinese Level 4 Test
- 居然 – jūrán: actually
- 口音 – kǒuyīn: accent
- 标准 – biāozhǔn: authentic
- 怕 – pà: to be afraid
- 下功夫 – xià gōngfu: to put in the effort
- 什么年纪 – shénme niánjì: any age, whatever age

问题/Questions

1. 劳拉是英国曼切斯特人。

   Laura is from Manchester, England.

   A. 对
   B. 错

2. 五十岁的时候，她决定改变她的生活方式。

   She decided to change her lifestyle when she was fifty years old.

   A. 对
   B. 错

3. 以下哪一项不适用于劳拉？

   Which of the following DOES NOT apply to Laura?

   A. 以前是老师
   B. 会说中文
   C. 有两个女儿
   D. 不会说马来文

4. 今年五月，劳拉没有考过汉语水平四级考试。

   Laura did not pass HSK level 4 in May this year.

   A. 对
   B. 错

5. 劳拉用马来文和朋友聊天一点儿问题也没有。

   Laura has no problem chatting with friends in Malay.

   A. 对
   B. 错

答案/Answers

1. B 错
   False

2. A 对
   True

3. D 不会说马来文
   Can't speak Malay

4. B 错
   False

5. A 对
   True

CHAPTER 16

智能手机 – SMARTPHONE

我听说最早的电话是在一八六六年**发明**的。在这一百五六十年的时间，电话已经从一个传统的**交流中介**发展成了我们生活中**不可缺少**的一个**多功能**的工具。

首先，电话**外观**的变化实在是太大了。从以前的**座机**到现在我们拿在手里的**手机**，它越来越小，可是功能越来越强。

通话和**发信息**还是电话**最基本**的功能。打电话的时候，现在我们常常用**视频**电话。每个星期，我都会给住在中国的父母打视频电话，跟他们聊聊天。

从这个世纪初，我们开始听见一个新名词：**智能手机**。 我们可以用智能手机**浏览网页**，**下载** app, 对我来说，最大的变化还是智能手机的**触摸屏**。我还记得 2007 年我第一次用手触摸苹果手机触摸屏的**感觉**。好**怪**啊！一两个月后我才开始**习惯**用触摸屏。

现在的智能手机就是一个**个人电脑**。我们在手机上听音乐、看电影、**付账单**和**订外卖**等等。智能手机**的确**为我们的生活提供了更大的**方便**。

智能手机可能是我们每个人最好的朋友。每天早上起床后，我们做的第一件事可能是看手机。每天晚上睡觉前，我们做的最后一件事可能也是看手机。

智能手机 – Smartphone
With English Translation

我听说最早的电话是在一八六六年**发明**的。在这一百五六十年的时间，电话已经从一个传统的**交流中介**发展成了我们生活中**不可缺少**的一个**多功能**的**工具**。

Wǒ tīng shuō zuìzǎo de diànhuà shì zài yībāliùliù nián **fāmíng** de. Zài zhè yìbǎi wǔliùshí nián de shíjiān, diànhuà yǐjīng cóng yígè chuántǒng de **jiāoliú zhōngjiè** fāzhǎn chéngle wǒmen shēnghuó zhōng **bùkě quēshǎo** de yígè **duō gōngnéng** de **gōngjù**.

I have heard that the first telephone was **invented** in 1866. In the past 150 or 160 years, the telephone has developed from a traditional **communication medium** to an **indispensable multifunctional tool** in our lives.

首先，电话**外观**的变化实在是太大了。从以前的**座机**到现在我们拿在手里的**手机**，它越来越小，可是功能越来越强。

Shǒuxiān, diànhuà **wàiguān** de biànhuà shízài shì tài dàle. Cóng yǐqián de **zuòjī** dào xiànzài wǒmen ná zài shǒu lǐ de **shǒujī**, tā yuè lái yuè xiǎo, kěshì gōngnéng yuè lái yuè qiáng.

First of all, the change in the **appearance** of the phone is simply huge. From the previous **landlines** to the **mobile phones** we hold in our hands, they are getting smaller and smaller, but their functions are getting more and more powerful.

通话和**发信息**还是电话**最基本**的功能。打电话的时候，现在我们常常用**视频**电话。每个星期，我都会给住在中国的父母打视频电话，跟他们聊聊天。

Tōnghuà hé **fā xìnxī** háishì diànhuà **zuì jīběn** de gōngnéng. Dǎ diànhuà de shíhou, xiànzài wǒmen chángcháng yòng **shìpín** diànhuà.

Měi gè xīngqī, wǒ dōu huì gěi zhù zài Zhōngguó de fùmǔ dǎ shìpín diànhuà, gēn tāmen liáo liáotiān.

Calling and **sending messages** are still the **most basic** functions of a phone. When making phone calls, nowadays we often use **video** calls. Every week, I make video calls with my parents who are living in China to chat with them.

从这个世纪初，我们开始听见一个新名词：**智能手机**。 我们可以用智能手机**浏览网页，下载** app。

Cóng zhège shìjì chū, wǒmen kāishǐ tīngjiàn yígè xīn míngcí: **Zhìnéng shǒujī.** Wǒmen kěyǐ yòng zhìnéng diànhuà **liúlǎn wǎngyè, xiàzài** app.

From the beginning of this century, we began to hear a new word: the **smartphone**. We can **browse web pages** and **download** apps to our smartphones.

对我来说，最大的变化还是智能手机的**触摸屏**。我还记得 2007 年我第一次用手触摸苹果手机触摸屏的**感觉**。好**怪**啊！一两个月后我才开始习**惯**用触摸屏。

Duì wǒ lái shuō, zuìdà de biànhuà hái shì zhìnéng shǒujī de **chùmōpíng.** Wǒ hái jìdé 2007 nián wǒ dìyī cì yòng shǒu chùmō píngguǒ shǒujī chùmō píng de **gǎnjué.** Hǎo **guài** a! Yì liǎng gè yuè hòu wǒ cái kāishǐ **xíguàn** yòng chùmō píng.

The biggest change for me is still the touchscreen of the smartphone. I still remember the first time I touched the **touchscreen** of an iPhone with my hand in 2007. How **strange**! It took me a month or two to **get used to** the touch screen.

现在的智能手机就是一个**个人电脑**。我们在手机上听音乐、看电影、**付账单**和**订外卖**等等。智能手机**的确**为我们的生活提供了更大的**方便**。

Xiànzài de zhìnéng shǒujī jiùshì yígè **gèrén diànnǎo**. Wǒmen zài shǒujī shàng tīng yīnyuè, kàn diànyǐng, **fù zhàngdān** hé **dìng wàimài** děng děng. Zhìnéng shǒujī **díquè** wèi wǒmen de shēnghuó tígōngle gèng dà de **fāngbiàn**.

Today's smartphone is a **personal computer**. We listen to music, watch movies, **pay bills, order takeout etc.** on our phones. Smartphones have **indeed** brought greater **convenience** to our lives.

智能手机可能是我们每个人最好的朋友。每天早上起床后，我们做的第一件事可能是看手机。每天晚上睡觉前，我们做的最后一件事可能也是看手机。

Zhìnéng shǒujī kěnéng shì wǒmen měi gè rén zuì hǎo de péngyǒu. Měitiān zǎoshang qǐchuáng hòu, wǒmen zuò de dìyī jiàn shì kěnéng shì kàn shǒujī. Měitiān wǎnshang shuìjiào qián, wǒmen zuò de zuìhòu yíjiàn shì kěnéng yěshì kàn shǒujī.

Smartphones are probably everyone's best friend. The first thing we do when we wake up in the morning is probably to look at our phones. The last thing we do every night before going to bed is probably to look at our phones too.

总结/Summary

智能手机是我们生活中不可缺少的一个工具。通话和发信息还是手机最基本的功能。打电话的时候，现在我们常常用视频电话。我们可以用智能手机浏览网页和下载 app。现在的智能手机就是一个个人电脑。我们在手机上听音乐、看电影、付账单和订外卖等等。智能手机为我们的生活提供了更大的方便。智能手机可能是我们每个人最好的朋友。每天早上起床后，我们做的第一件事可能是看手机。每天晚上睡觉前，我们做的最后一件事可能也是看手机。

Zhìnéng shǒujī shì wǒmen shēnghuó zhōng bù kě quēshǎo de yígè gōngjù. Tōnghuà hé fā xìnxī háishì shǒujī zuì jīběn de gōngnéng. Dǎ diànhuà de shíhou, xiànzài wǒmen chángcháng yòng shìpín diànhuà. Wǒmen kěyǐ yòng zhìnéng shǒujī liúlǎn wǎngyè hé xiàzài app. Xiànzài de zhìnéng shǒujī jiùshì yígè gèrén diànnǎo. Wǒmen zài shǒujī shàng tīng yīnyuè, kàn diànyǐng, fù zhàngdān hé dìng wàimài děng děng. Zhìnéng shǒujī wèi wǒmen de shēnghuó tígōngle gèng dà de fāngbiàn. Zhìnéng shǒujī kěnéng shì wǒmen měi gè rén zuì hǎo de péngyǒu. Měitiān zǎoshang qǐchuáng hòu, wǒmen zuò de dìyī jiàn shì kěnéng shì kàn shǒujī. Měitiān wǎnshang shuìjiào qián, wǒmen zuò de zuìhòu yíjiàn shì kěnéng yěshì kàn shǒujī.

Smartphones are an indispensable tool in our lives. Calling and sending messages are still the most basic functions of a mobile phone. When making phone calls, nowadays we often use video calls. We can browse the web and download apps with our smartphones. Today's smartphone is a personal computer. We listen to music, watch movies, pay bills, order takeout etc. on our phones. Smartphones have brought greater convenience to our lives. A smartphone may be everyone's best friend. The first thing we probably do when we wake up in the morning is to look at our phones. The last thing we probably do every night before going to bed is also to look at our phones.

生词/Vocabulary List

- 发明 – fāmíng: invention
- 交流 – jiāoliú: to communicate
- 中介 – zhōngjiè: medium
- 不可缺少 – bùkě quēshǎo: indispensable
- 多功能 – duō gōngnéng: multifunction
- 工具 – gōngjù: tool
- 外观 – wàiguān: appearance
- 座机 – zuòjī: landline
- 手机 – shǒujī: cell phone
- 通话 – tōnghuà: to call, call
- 发信息 – fā xìnxī: to send message
- 最基本 – zuì jīběn: the most basic
- 视频 – shìpín: video
- 智能手机 – zhìnéng shǒujī: smartphone
- 浏览 – liúlǎn: to browse
- 网页 – wǎngyè: web page
- 下载 – xiàzài: to download
- 触摸 – chùmō: to touch
- 屏 – píng: screen
- 感觉 – gǎnjué: to feel, feel
- 怪 – guài: strange
- 习惯 – xíguàn: to get used to
- 个人电脑 – gèrén diànnǎo: personal computer
- 付账单 – fù zhàngdān: to pay bills
- 订外卖 – dìng wàimài: to order takeout
- 的确 – díquè: indeed
- 方便 – fāngbiàn: convenient

问题/**Questions**

1. 最早的电话是在一八六六年发明的。

   The first telephone was invented in 1866.

   A. 对
   B. 错

2. 通话和发信息已经不是电话最基本的功能。

   Calling and texting are no longer the most basic functions of a phone.

   A. 对
   B. 错

3. 我多长时间才开始习惯用触摸屏？

   How long did it take me to get used to using a touchscreen?

   A. 一两个星期
   B. 一两个月
   C. 两三个月
   D. 半年

4. 以下哪一项不适用于智能手机？

   Which one of the following doesn't apply to smartphones？

   A. 听音乐
   B. 看电影
   C. 订外卖
   D. 做作业

5. 智能手机可能是我们每个人最好的朋友。

   A smartphone may be everyone's best friend.

   A. 对
   B. 错

答案/Answers

1. A 对
   True

2. B 错
   False

3. B 一两个月
   One to two months

4. D 做作业
   Do homework

5. A 对
   True

CHAPTER 17

网购的好处和坏处 – PROS AND CONS OF ONLINE SHOPPING

现代人的生活是越来越**方便**了！就**拿网购来说吧**，坐在沙发上，**鼠标一点，送货上门，省时省力**。你觉得网购**十全十美**吗？今天我们就来**讨论**讨论。

如果你买一些**日常**生活用品，比如说，牛奶、**洗衣粉、卫生纸**等等，你已经知道买哪些**品牌**的，也知道哪里的最便宜，在网上买这些用品是非常**合适**的。你可以**节约**很多时间和**力气**，也可以买到最便宜的。买衣服就不太一样了！买衣服的时候需要**试**一试，看看**材料**的**质量**怎么样，因为这些**原因**，所以我不常常在网上买穿的。还有的时候，商家会给你**寄来**不对的商品，当然了，这种**情况**很少**发生**，可是如果发生了，你就需要联系商家，然后**安排**把东西**邮**回去。

网购也有一些**普遍**的**麻烦事**。现在所有的网店都需要**用户注册**，注册的时候用户要选择**密码**。可以**想象**得到，有时候我们会**忘记**密码。我们每个人最少都会在一二十个网店上买东西，所以要**正确**地记住所有的密码也是一件需要**用心**的事情。用户注册**成功**后，网店需要**安全**地保护用户的信息，可是**不幸的**是有时候**黑客**会进入网店的电脑**系统窥视**用户信息。用户一些很**敏感**的信息，比如说：**家庭地址，电话号码**和**银行账户**等等都会变得不安全。

全面来看，网购的好处还是大大地高于网购的坏处的。

网购的好处和坏处 – Pros and Cons of Online Shopping With English Translation

现代人的生活是越来越**方便**了！就**拿网购来说吧**，坐在沙发上，**鼠标一点**，**送货上门**，**省时省力**。你觉得网购**十全十美**吗？今天我们就来**讨论**讨论。

Xiàndài rén de shēnghuó shì yuè lái yuè **fāngbiàn**le! Jiù **ná wǎng gòu lái shuō ba**, zuò zài shāfā shàng, **shǔbiāo** yìdiǎn, **sòng huò shàngmén**, **shěng shí shěng lì**. Nǐ juéde wǎng gòu **shíquánshíměi** ma? Jīntiān wǒmen jiù lái **tǎolùn** tǎolùn.

Modern life is becoming more and more **convenient**! **Take online shopping**, for example: sit on the sofa, **click** the **mouse**, and **have it delivered to your door, saving time and effort**. Do you think online shopping is **perfect**? Today we are going to **discuss** that.

如果你买一些**日常**生活用品，比如说，牛奶、**洗衣粉**、**卫生纸**等等，你已经知道买哪些**品牌**的，也知道哪里的最便宜，在网上买这些用品是非常**合适**的。

Rúguǒ nǐ mǎi yìxiē **rìcháng** shēnghuó yòngpǐn, bǐrú shuō, niúnǎi, **xǐyīfěn**, **wèishēngzhǐ** děng děng, nǐ yǐjīng zhīdào mǎi nǎxiē **pǐnpái** de, yě zhīdào nǎlǐ de zuì piányi, zài wǎngshàng mǎi zhèxiē yòngpǐn shì fēicháng **héshì** de.

If you buy some **daily** necessities, such as milk, **detergent**, **toilet paper**, and others, you already know which **brands** to buy and where the cheapest ones are. It is **fine** to buy these online.

你可以**节约**很多时间和**力气**，也可以买到最便宜的。买衣服就不太一样了！买衣服的时候需要**试**一试，看看**材料**的**质量**怎么样，因为这些**原因**，所以我不常常在网上买穿的。

Nǐ kěyǐ **jiéyuē** hěnduō shíjiān hé lìqi, yě kěyǐ mǎi dào zuì piányi de. Mǎi yīfu jiù bú tài yíyàng le! Mǎi yīfu de shíhou xūyào **shì** yi shì, kàn kan **cáiliào** de **zhìliàng** zěnme yàng, yīnwèi zhèxiē **yuányīn**, suǒyǐ wǒ bù chángcháng zài wǎngshàng mǎi chuān de.

You can **save** a lot of time and **effort**, and you can also buy the cheapest item. Shopping for clothes is not the same! When shopping for clothes, you need to **try** them **on**, to see the **quality** of the **material**, and for these **reasons** I don't often buy clothes online.

还有的时候，**商家**会给你**寄来**不对的商品，当然了，这种**情况**很少**发生**，可是如果发生了，你就需要联系商家，然后**安排**把东西邮回去。

Hái yǒu de shíhou, shāngjiā huì gěi nǐ **jì lái** bú duì de shāngpǐn, dāngrán le, zhè zhǒng **qíngkuàng** hěn shǎo **fāshēng**, kěshì rúguǒ fāshēngle, nǐ jiù xūyào liánxì shāngjiā, ránhòu **ānpái** bǎ dōngxi **yóu huíqù**.

Other times, the **merchant** will **send** you the wrong item; of course, **this** rarely **happens**, but if it happens, you need to contact the merchant and **arrange** for the item to be **returned**.

网购也有一些**普遍**的**麻烦事**。现在所有的网店都需要**用户注册**，注册的时候用户要选择**密码**。可以**想象**得到，有时候我们会**忘记**密码。

Wǎng gòu yě yǒu yìxiē **pǔbiàn** de **máfan shì**. Xiànzài suǒyǒu de wǎng diàn dōu xūyào **yònghù zhùcè**, zhùcè de shíhou yònghù yào xuǎnzé **mìmǎ**. Kěyǐ **xiǎngxiàng** de dào, yǒu shíhou wǒmen huì **wàngjì** mìmǎ.

Online shopping also has some **common hassles**. All online stores now require **user registration**, and users need to choose a **password** when registering. As you can **imagine**, sometimes we will **forget** our passwords.

我们每个人最少都会在一二十个网店上买东西，所以要**正确**地记住所有的密码也是一件需要**用心**的事情。

Wǒmen měi gè rén zuìshǎo dōu huì zài yī'èrshí gè wǎng diàn shàng mǎi dōngxi, suǒyǐ yào **zhèngquè** de jì zhù suǒyǒu de mìmǎ yěshì yíjiàn xūyào **yòngxīn** de shìqing.

Every one of us buys from at least ten or twenty online stores, so remembering all the passwords **correctly** requires some level of **attention**.

用户注册**成功**后，网店需要**安全**地保护用户的信息，可是**不幸的**是有时候**黑客**会进入网店的电脑**系统窥视**用户信息。

Yònghù zhùcè **chénggōng** hòu, wǎng diàn xūyào **ānquán** de bǎohù yònghù de xìnxī, kěshì **búxìng de** shì yǒu shíhou **hēikè** huì jìnrù wǎng diàn de diànnǎo **xìtǒng kuīshì** yònghù xìnxī.

After the user is **successfully** registered, the online store needs to **safely** protect the user's information; **unfortunately** sometimes **hackers** will enter the online store's computer **system** to **look into** the user's information.

用户一些很**敏感**的信息，比如说：**家庭地址**，**电话号码**和**银行账户**等等都会变得不安全。

Yònghù yìxiē hěn **mǐngǎn** de xìnxī, bǐrú shuō: **Jiātíng dìzhǐ, diànhuà hàomǎ** hé **yínháng zhànghù** děng děng dōu huì biàn dé bù ānquán.

Some of the user's **sensitive** information, such as **home address**, **phone number**, and **bank account**, will become insecure.

全面来看，网购的好处还是大大地多于网购的坏处的。

Quánmiàn lái kàn, wǎng gòu de hǎochù háishì dàdà de duōyú wǎng gòu de huàichu de.

Overall, the advantages of online shopping are still much greater than the disadvantages of online shopping.

总结/Summary

今天我们就来讨论网购。你觉得网购十全十美吗？买一些日常生活用品网购是非常合适的。你可以节约很多时间和力气，也可以买到最便宜的。买衣服就不太一样了！如果商家给你寄来不对的商品，你需要联系商家，然后安排把东西邮回去。网购也有一些普遍的麻烦事，比如说：用户注册和选择密码等等。网店需要安全地保护用户的信息，可是不幸的是有时候黑客会进入网店的电脑系统窥视用户信息。全面来看，网购的好处还是大大地多于网购的坏处的。

Jīntiān wǒmen jiù lái tǎolùn wǎng gòu. Nǐ juédé wǎng gòu shíquánshíměi ma? Mǎi yìxiē rìcháng shēnghuó yòngpǐn wǎng gòu shì fēicháng héshì de. Nǐ kěyǐ jiéyuē hěnduō shíjiān hé lìqi, yě kěyǐ mǎi dào zuì piányi de. Mǎi yīfu jiù bú tài yíyàng le! Rúguǒ shāngjiā gěi nǐ jì lái bú duì de shāngpǐn, nǐ xūyào liánxì shāngjiā, ránhòu ānpái bǎ dōngxi yóu huíqù. Wǎng gòu yě yǒu yìxiē pǔbiàn de máfan shì, bǐrú shuō: Yònghù zhùcè hé xuǎnzé mìmǎ děng děng. Wǎng diàn xūyào ānquán de bǎohù yònghù de xìnxī, kěshì bùxìng de shì yǒu shíhou hēikè huì jìnrù wǎng diàn de diànnǎo xìtǒng kuīshì yònghù xìnxī. Quánmiàn lái kàn, wǎng gòu de hǎochù háishì dàdà de duōyú wǎng gòu de huàichu de.

Today we are going to discuss online shopping. Do you think online shopping is perfect? It is fine to buy some daily necessities online. You can save a lot of time and effort, and you can also buy the cheapest item. Shopping for clothes is not the same! If the merchant sent you the wrong item, you would need to contact them and arrange for the item to be returned. Online shopping also has some common hassles, such as: user registration and password selection, and so on. Online stores need to securely protect users' information;

198

unfortunately sometimes hackers can hack into the online store's computer system to look into users' information. Overall, the advantages of online shopping far outweigh the disadvantages of online shopping.

生词/Vocabulary List

- 方便 – fāngbiàn: convenient
- 拿...来说吧 – ná...lái shuō ba: take ... for example
- 网购 – wǎng gòu: online shopping
- 鼠标 – shǔbiāo: mouse
- 点 – diǎn: to click
- 送货上门 – sòng huò shàngmén: doorstep delivery
- 省时省力 – shěng shí shěng lì: save time and effort
- 十全十美 – shíquánshíměi: perfect
- 讨论 – tǎolùn: to discuss
- 日常 – rìcháng: daily
- 洗衣粉 – xǐyīfěn: detergent
- 卫生纸 – wèishēngzhǐ: toilet paper
- 品牌 – pǐnpái: brand
- 合适 – héshì: fine, suitable
- 节约 – jiéyuē: to save
- 力气 – lìqi: energy
- 试 – shì: to try
- 材料 – cáiliào: material
- 质量 – zhìliàng: quality
- 原因 – yuányīn: reason
- 寄来 – jì lái: to send over
- 情况 – qíngkuàng: situation, circumstances
- 发生 – fāshēng: to occur, to happen
- 安排 – ānpái: to arrange
- 邮回去 – yóu huíqù: to post back
- 普遍 – pǔbiàn: common
- 麻烦事 – máfan shì: trouble
- 用户 – yònghù: user
- 注册 – zhùcè: to register
- 密码 – mìmǎ: password
- 想象 – xiǎngxiàng: imagine
- 忘记 – wàngjì: to forget
- 正确 – zhèngquè: correct
- 用心 – yòng xīn: pay attention to
- 成功 – chénggōng: success
- 安全 – ānquán: safe, safety
- 不幸的 – búxìng de: unfortunately
- 黑客 – hēikè: hacker
- 系统 – xìtǒng: system
- 窥视 – kuīshì: to look into
- 敏感 – mǐngǎn: sensitive

- 家庭住址 – jiātíng zhùzhǐ: home address
- 电话号码 – diànhuà hàomǎ: phone number
- 银行账户 – yínháng zhànghù: bank account
- 全面来看 – quánmiàn lái kàn: overall

问题/Questions

1. 网购是十全十美的。

   Online shopping is perfect.

   A. 对
   B. 错

2. 在网上买一些日常生活用品是很合适的。

   It is fine to buy some daily necessities online.

   A. 对
   B. 错

3. 以下哪项不适用于网购用户？

   Which of the following does not apply to the online shopping user?

   A. 用户注册
   B. 选择密码
   C. 记住密码
   D. 保护信息

4. 黑客从来不能进入网店的电脑系统。

   Hackers can never get into the computer system of an online store.

   A. 对
   B. 错

5. 全面来看，网购的好处大大多于网购的坏处。

   Overall, the advantages of online shopping far outweigh the disadvantages of online shopping.

   A. 对
   B. 错

答案/Answers

1. B 错
   False

2. A 对
   True

3. D 保护信息
   To protect information

4. B 错
   False

5. A 对
   True

CHAPTER 18

伦敦的格林尼治区 –
LONDON'S GREENWICH

如果你有机会来英国伦敦旅游，你一定要到**格林尼治**区看一看。

格林尼治，**原译格林威治，** 是英国**大伦敦**的一个区。格林尼治区位于伦敦东南、泰晤士河南**岸**。格林尼治的**小镇**是一个有丰富的历史和地方**特色**的小镇，在这里你可以体验到集**天文、航海、皇室、市集**于一体的格林尼治，**加上位于**北格林尼治的**全球瞩目**的**千禧巨蛋**，格林尼治区**绝对**是到伦敦**不容错过**的一日之旅。

格林威治的名字一定让你想起格林威治**天文台**了吧？格林威治因**其**天文台而**闻名于世**。

早在**公元 1675** 年，英王**查理二世**就决定在格林威治山**顶**建立英国皇家天文台。公元 1767 年，经过几十年的**研究**，格林威治的皇家天文学家们**制成**了世界上第一张**海图**。英国的**海员**可以**根据**星星的**位置确定**船的**方位**。你上中学地理课的时候也许学过：从公元 1884 年，世界以通过格林威治天文台的**经线**为**本初子午线**，**即零度经线**，以**此计算**地球上的**经度**；以格林威治为世界**时区**的**起点**；以格林威治的天文台的**计时仪器**来**校准**时间。

伦敦的格林尼治区– London's Greenwich

With English Translation

如果你有机会来英国伦敦旅游，你一定要到**格林尼治区**看一看。

Rúguǒ nǐ yǒu jīhuì lái Yīngguó Lúndūn lǚyóu, nǐ yídìng yào dào **Gélínnízhì qū** kàn yi kàn.

If you have the chance to visit London, England, you must visit **Greenwich**.

格林尼治，**原译格林威治**， 是英国**大伦敦**的一个区。格林尼治区位于伦敦东南、泰晤士河南**岸**。格林尼治的**小镇**是一个有丰富的历史和地方**特色**的小镇。

Gélínnízhì, **yuán yì Gélínwēizhì**, shì Yīngguó **Dàlúndūn** de yígè qū. Gélínnízhì qū wèiyú Lúndūn dōngnán, Tàiwùshìhé nán **àn**. Gélínnízhì de **xiǎo zhèn** shì yígè yǒu fēngfù de lìshǐ hé dìfāng **tèsè** de xiǎo zhèn.

Greenwich is a district in **Greater London**, UK. Greenwich is located in southeast London, on the south **bank** of the river Thames. The **town** of Greenwich is a town with rich history and local **features**.

在这里你可以体验到**集天文**、**航海**、**皇室**、**市集**于一体的格林尼治，加上位于北格林尼治的**全球瞩目**的**千禧巨蛋**，格林尼治区**绝对**是到伦敦**不容错过**的一日之旅。

Zài zhèlǐ nǐ kěyǐ tǐyàn dào **jí tiānwén, hánghǎi, huángshì, shì jí** yú **yìtǐ** de Gélínnízhì, **jiā shàng wèiyú** běi Gélínnízhì de **quánqiú zhǔmù** de **Qiānxǐjùdàn**, Gélínnízhì qū **juéduì** shì dào Lúndūn **bùróng cuòguò** de yí rì zhī lǚ.

Here you can experience **astronomy, navigation, royalty**, and **markets all in one go**, plus the **world-renowned Millennium Dome** in North Greenwich, Greenwich is **definitely** an **unmissable** day trip when coming to London.

格林威治的名字一定让你想起格林威治**天文台**了吧？格林威治因**其**天文台而**闻名于世**。

Gélínwēizhì de míngzì yídìng ràng nǐ xiǎngqǐ Gélínwēizhì **tiānwéntái** le ba? Gélínwēizhì yīn **qí** tiānwéntái ér **wénmíng yú shì**.

The name Greenwich must remind you of the Greenwich **Observatory**, right? Greenwich is **famous** for **its** observatory.

早在**公元** 1675 年，英王**查理二世**就决定在格林威治山**顶**建立英国皇家天文台。公元 1767 年，经过几十年的**研究**，格林威治的皇家天文学家们**制成**了世界上第一张**海图**。英国的**海员**可以**根据**星星的**位置确定**船的**方位**。

Zǎo zài **gōngyuán** 1675 nián, yīng wáng **Chálǐ Èrshì** jiù juédìng zài Gélínwēi zhì shān**dǐng** jiànlì Yīngguó Huángjiā Tiānwéntái. Gōngyuán 1767 nián, jīngguò jǐ shí nián de **yánjiū**, Gélínwēizhì de huángjiā tiānwénxuéjiā men **zhì chéng**le shìjiè shàng dìyī zhāng **hǎitú**. Yīngguó de **hǎiyuán** kěyǐ **gēnjù** xīngxīng de **wèizhì quèdìng** chuán de **fāngwèi**.

As early as 1675 **CE**, King **Charles II** of England decided to build the Royal Observatory on the **top** of a Greenwich hill. In 1767 CE, after decades of **research**, the Royal Astronomers at Greenwich **produced** the world's first **sea map**. British **sailors** could **define** the ship's **location** based on the **position** of the stars.

你上中学地理课的时候也许学过：从公元 1884 年起，世界以通过格林威治天文台的**经线**为**本初子午线**，即零度经线，以**此计算**地球上的**经度**；以格林威治为世界**时区**的**起点**；以格林威治的天文台的**计时仪器**来**校准**时间。

Nǐ shàng zhōngxué dìlǐ kè de shíhou yěxǔ xuéguò: cóng gōngyuán 1884 nián qǐ, shìjiè yǐ tōngguò Gélínwēizhì Tiānwéntái de **jīngxiàn** wéi **Běnchū Zǐwǔxiàn, jí língdù jīngxiàn**, yǐ **cǐ jìsuàn** dìqiú shàng de **jīngdù**;

yǐ Gélínwēizhì wéi shìjiè **shíqū** de **qǐdiǎn**; yǐ Gélínwēizhì de tiānwéntái de **jìshí yíqì** lái **jiàozhǔn** shíjiān.

You may have learned in your secondary school geography lesson: since 1884 CE, the world uses the **longitude** passing through the Greenwich Observatory as the **meridian, or the zero-degree longitude**, to **calculate longitude** on the earth; Greenwich time is the **starting point** of the world **time zone**; the **timekeeping instruments** of the Observatory in Greenwich are used to **calibrate** time worldwide.

总结/Summary

格林尼治，原译格林威治，是英国大伦敦的一个区。格林尼治的小镇是一个有丰富的历史和地方特色的小镇，在这里你可以体验到集天文、航海、皇室、市集于一体的格林尼治，全球瞩目的千禧巨蛋位于北格林尼治。格林威治因其天文台而闻名于世。公元1675 年，英王查理二世决定在格林威治山顶建立英国皇家天文台。公元 1884 年，世界以通过格林威治天文台的经线为本初子午线，即零度经线，以此计算地球上的经度；以格林威治为世界时区的起点；以格林威治的天文台的计时仪器来校准时间。

Gélínnízhì, yuán yì Gélínwēizhì, shì Yīngguó Dàlúndūn de yígè qū. Gélínnízhì de xiǎo zhèn shì yígè yǒu fēngfù de lìshǐ hé dìfāng tèsè de xiǎo zhèn, zài zhèlǐ nǐ kěyǐ tǐyàn dào jí tiānwén, hánghǎi, huángshì, shìjí yú yìtǐ de Gélínnízhì, quánqiú zhǔmù de Qiānxǐjùdàn wèiyú běi Gélínnízhì. Gélínwēizhì yīn qí tiānwéntái ér wénmíng yú shì. Gōngyuán 1675 nián, yīng wáng Chálǐ Èrshì juédìng zài Gélínwēizhì shāndǐng jiànlì Yīngguó Huángjiā Tiānwéntái. Gōngyuán 1884 nián, shìjiè yǐ tōngguò Gélínwēizhì Tiānwéntái de jīngxiàn wéi Běnchū Zǐwǔxiàn, jí língdù jīngxiàn, yǐ cǐ jìsuàn dìqiú shàng de jīngdù; yǐ Gélínwēizhì wéi shìjiè shíqū de qǐdiǎn; yǐ Gélínwēizhì de tiānwéntái de jìshí yíqì lái jiàozhǔn shíjiān.

Greenwich is a district in Greater London, England. The town of Greenwich is a town with rich history and local characteristics. Here you can experience astronomy, navigation, royalty and markets all in one go. The world-renowned Millennium Dome is located in North Greenwich. Greenwich is world famous for its observatory. In 1675, King Charles II of England decided to build the Royal Observatory on the top of a Greenwich hill. In 1884 CE, the world took the longitude passing through the Greenwich Observatory as the meridian, that is, the zero-degree longitude, to calculate longitudes on the earth. Greenwich time is the starting point of the world time zone, and the timing instruments of the Greenwich Observatory are used to calibrate time worldwide.

生词/Vocabulary List

- 格林尼治 – Gélínnízhì: Greenwich
- 原译 – yuán yì: original translation
- 大伦敦 – Dàlúndūn: Greater London
- 岸 – àn: shore
- 小镇 – xiǎo zhèn: small town
- 特色 – tèsè: characteristic, features
- 集...于一体 – jí...yú yìtǐ: all in one
- 天文 – tiānwén: astronomy
- 航海 – hánghǎi: navigation
- 皇室 – huángshì: royal family
- 市集 – shì jí: market
- 加上 – jiā shàng: plus
- 位于 – wèiyú: to situate
- 全球瞩目 – quánqiú zhǔmù: global attention, world-renowned
- 千禧巨蛋 – Qiānxǐjùdàn: Millennium Dome, O2
- 绝对 – juéduì: absolute
- 不容错过 – bùróng cuòguò: should not be missed
- 天文台 – tiānwéntái: observatory
- 其 – qí: it, its
- 闻名于世 – wénmíng yú shì: world famous
- 公元 – gōngyuán: CE
- 查理二世 – Chálǐ Èrshì: Charles II
- 顶 – dǐng: top
- 研究 – yánjiū: to research, research
- 制成 – zhì chéng: to produce
- 海图 – hǎi tú: sea map
- 海员 – hǎiyuán: sailor
- 根据 – gēnjù: according to
- 位置 – wèizhì: location
- 确定 – quèdìng: to define,
- 方位 – fāngwèi: position
- 经线 – jīngxiàn: longitude
- 本初子午线 – Běnchūzǐwǔxiàn: meridian
- 即 – jí: that is, i.e.
- 零度经线 – língdù jīngxiàn: zero degree longitude
- 此 – cǐ: this
- 计算 – jìsuàn: to calculate
- 经度 – jīngdù: longitude

- 时区– shíqū: time zone
- 起点 – qǐdiǎn: starting point
- 计时 – jìshí: timing
- 仪器 – yíqì: instrument
- 校准 – jiàozhǔn: to calibrate

问题/Questions

1. 格林尼治区在伦敦的西北。

   Greenwich is in the northwest of London.

   A. 对
   B. 错

2. 在格林尼治没有市场。

   There is no market in Greenwich.

   A. 对
   B. 错

3. 千禧巨蛋在南格林尼治。

   The Millennium Dome (O2) is in South Greenwich.

   A. 对
   B. 错

4. 格林尼治天文台是在公元 1675 年建立的。

   The Greenwich Observatory was established in 1675 CE.

   A. 对
   B. 错

5. 通过格林尼治天文台的经线是本初子午线。

   The longitude passing through Greenwich Observatory is the meridian.

   A. 对
   B. 错

答案/Answers

1. B 错
   False

2. B 错
   False

3. B 错
   False

4. A 对
   True

5. A 对
   True

CHAPTER 19

美国的感恩节和中国的双十一 –
THANKSGIVING IN THE UNITED STATES AND DOUBLE ELEVEN IN CHINA

大家熟知的西方的**感恩节**是一个文化**传统**，它起源于北美**土著习俗**。**长期**以来被视为一个有趣的**世俗**的节日。在**欧洲**人到来之前的几个**世纪**里，北美的土著居民**实践**了**早期形式**的感恩节。 这是一种**感谢丰收**的方式。 当英国**殖民者**在 17 世纪初**抵达**现在的美国时，他们也**采用**了这一传统。虽然**日期**不同，但现在美国、加拿大、格林纳达、圣卢西亚和利比里亚都**庆祝**感恩节。

传统上，感恩节是庆祝一年中的**祝福**，包括**丰收**的节日。 在感恩节期间，美国人**通常**会**共享**家庭**聚餐**和**观看特殊**的**体育赛事**。现在它已经**演变**成为一个**大规模**的商业活动。在美国，感恩节是在十一月的第四个星期四。感恩节的下一天是**著名**的黑色星期五。黑色星期五在传统上**标志**着美国圣诞购物季的开始。在这一天，许多商店和**商场**开始同时在**线上线下打折**，并且经常提早开门。一些商店的**打折**将持续到下星期一（ "网络星期一" ）或整整一周（"网络周"）。

近十年来，每年十一月在中国也有一个**大型**的**火热**的打折**促销**活动。**阿里巴巴旗**下的**淘宝**商城**仿照类似**美国感恩节大促销，在 2009 年 11 月 11 日推出了以"全场五折，全国**包邮**"作为促销口**号**的"淘宝商城促销日"。在被**业界**认为传统销售**淡季**的 11 月，淘宝商城**交易额突破** 5200 万元，是当时**日常**交易额的 10 **倍**。2012

年 11 月 11 日网络购物全日销售额**超过**美国网络星期一，成为全球最大的**互联网**购物节日。

美国的感恩节和中国的双十一 – Thanksgiving in the United States and Double Eleven in China
With English Translation

大家**熟知**的西方的**感恩节**是一个文化**传统**，它**起源**于北美**土著**习**俗**。**长期**以来被**视为**一个有趣的**世俗**的节日。

Dàjiā **shúzhī** de xīfāng de **gǎn'ēn jié** shì yīgè wénhuà **chuántǒng**, tā **qǐyuán** yú běiměi **tǔzhù xísú. Chángqī** yǐlái bèi **shì wéi** yīgè yǒuqù de **shìsú** de jiérì.

The **well-known** Western **Thanksgiving** is a cultural tradition，it **originated** in North American Indigenous practices. It has **long** been **regarded** as a fun, secular holiday.

在**欧洲**人到来之前的几个**世纪**里，北美的土著居民**实践**了**早期形**式的感恩节。这是一种**感谢丰收**的方式。当英国**殖民者**在 17 世纪初**抵达**现在的美国时，他们也**采用**了这一传统。

Zài **ōuzhōu** rén dàolái zhīqián de jǐ gè **shìjì** lǐ, běiměi de tǔzhù jūmín **shíjiàn**le **zǎoqī xíngshì** de gǎn'ēn jié. Zhè shì yī zhǒng **gǎnxiè fēngshōu** de fāngshì. Dāng yīngguó **zhímín zhě** zài shí qī shìjì chū **dǐdá** xiànzài dì měiguó shí, tāmen yě **cǎiyòng**le zhè yī chuántǒng.

An early form of Thanksgiving was practiced by the Indigenous peoples of North America for centuries before the arrival of Europeans. It was a way of giving thanks for the harvest. When British colonists arrived in what is now the United States in the early seventeenth century, they adopted the tradition as well.

虽然**日期**不同，但现在美国、加拿大、格林纳达、圣卢西亚和利比里亚都**庆祝**感恩节。

Suīrán **rìqī** bùtóng, dàn xiànzài měiguó, jiānádà, gélínnàdá, shèng lú xīyǎ hé lìbǐlǐyǎ dōu **qìngzhù** gǎn'ēn jié.

Although the **dates** are different, Thanksgiving is now **celebrated** in the United States, Canada, Grenada, Saint Lucia, and Liberia.

传统上，感恩节是庆祝一年中的**祝福**，包括丰收的节日。 在感恩节期间，美国人**通常**会**共享**家庭**聚餐**和**观看特殊**的**体育赛事**。

Chuántǒng shàng, gǎn'ēn jié shì qìngzhù yī nián zhōng de **zhùfú**, bāokuò **fēngshōu** de jiérì. Zài gǎn'ēn jié qíjiān, měiguó rén **tōngcháng** huì **gòngxiǎng** jiātíng **jùcān** hé **guānkàn tèshū** de **tǐyù sàishì**.

Traditionally, Thanksgiving is a holiday that celebrates the **blessings** of the year, including a good **harvest**. During Thanksgiving, Americans **typically share** family **meals** and **watch special sporting events**.

现在它已经**演变**成为一个**大规模**的商业活动。在美国，感恩节是在十一月的第四个星期四。感恩节的下一天是**著名**的黑色星期五。

Xiànzài tā yǐjīng yǎnbiàn chéngwéi yígè **dà guīmó** de shāngyè huódòng. Zài Měiguó, Gǎn'ēnjié shì zài shíyī yuè de dìsì gè xīngqīsì. Gǎn'ēnjié de xià yītiān shì **zhùmíng** de Hēisè Xīngqīwǔ.

Now it has **evolved** into a **large-scale** commercial event. In the United States, Thanksgiving falls on the fourth Thursday in November. The day after Thanksgiving is the **famous** Black Friday.

黑色星期五在传统上**标志**着美国圣诞购物季的开始。在这一天，许多商店和**商场**开始同时**在线上线下打折**，并且经常提早开门。

Hēisè Xīngqīwǔ zài chuántǒng shàng **biāozhì**zhe Měiguó Shèngdàn gòuwù jì de kāishǐ. Zài zhè yītiān, xǔduō shāngdiàn hé **shāngchǎng** kāishǐ tóngshí zài **xiànshàng xiànxià dǎzhé**, bìngqiě jīngcháng tízǎo kāimén.

Black Friday traditionally **marks** the start of the Christmas shopping season in the United States. On this day, many stores and **malls** start

the sales online and offline at the same time, often opening their doors early.

一些商店的打折将持续到下星期一（"网络星期一"）或整整一周（"网络周"）。

Yìxiē shāngdiàn de dǎzhé jiāng chíxù dào xià xīngqīyī ("**Wǎngluò Xīngqīyī**") huò zhěngzhěng yìzhōu ("Wǎngluò Zhōu").

Some store sales will continue until the next Monday ("**Cyber Monday**") or for a full week ("Cyber Week").

近十年来，每年十一月在中国也有一个**大型**的**火热**的打折**促销**活动。

Jìn shí nián lái, měi nián shíyī yuè zài Zhōngguó yě yǒu yígè **dàxíng** de **huǒrè** de dǎzhé **cùxiāo** huódòng.

For the past ten years, there has also been a **large** and **popular** sale **promotion** in China every November.

阿里巴巴旗下的**淘宝**商城**仿照类似**美国感恩节大促销，在 2009 年 11 月 11 日推出了以"全场五折，全国**包邮**"作为促销口号的"淘宝商城促销日"。

Ālǐbābā qíxià de **Táobǎo** shāngchéng **fǎngzhào lèisì** Měiguó Gǎn'ēnjié dà cùxiāo, zài 2009 nián 11 yuè 11 rì tuīchūle yǐ "quán chǎng wǔ zhé, quánguó **bāo yóu**" zuòwéi cùxiāo **kǒuhào** de "táobǎo shāngchéng cùxiāo rì".

Taobao Mall, a **subsidiary** of **Alibaba**, **imitated** a **similar** American Thanksgiving promotion, and launched the "Taobao Mall Promotion Day" on November 11, 2009, with "50% off everything, **free shipping** nationwide" as the promotion **slogan**.

在被**业界**认为传统销售**淡季**的 11 月，淘宝商城**交易额突破** 5200 万元，是当时日常交易额的 10 倍。

Zài bèi **yèjiè** rènwéi chuántǒng xiāoshòu **dànjì** de 11 yuè, táobǎo shāngchéng **jiāoyì é tūpò** 5200 **wàn** yuán, shì dāngshí **rìcháng** jiāoyì é de 10 **bèi**.

In November, which is considered a traditional **off-season** by the **industry**, the **transaction volume** of Taobao Mall **exceeded** 52 million yuan, which was 10 **times** the **daily** transaction volume at that time.

2012 年 11 月 11 日网络购物全日销售额**超过**美国网络星期一，成为全球最大的**互联网**购物节日。

2012 Nián 11 yuè 11 rì wǎngluò gòuwù quánrì xiāoshòu é **chāoguò** Měiguó Wǎngluò Xīngqīyī, chéngwéi quánqiú zuìdà de **hùliánwǎng** gòuwù jiérì.

On November 11, 2012, the full-day sales of online shopping **surpassed** Cyber Monday in the United States, becoming the world's busiest **Internet** shopping day.

总结/Summary

西方的感恩节是一个文化传统，它起源于北美土著习俗，同时也是一个世俗的节日。在感恩节，美国人通常会共享家庭聚餐和观看特殊的体育赛事。现在它已经演变成为一个大规模的商业活动。在这一天，许多商店和商场开始同时在线上线下打折。一些商店的打折会一直持续到网络周。十一月在中国也有一个大型的火热的打折促销活动。淘宝商城在 2009 年 11 月 11 日推出了以"全场五折，全国包邮"作为促销口号的"淘宝商城促销日"。淘宝商城交易额突破 5200 万元。2012 年 11 月 11 日网络购物全日销售额超过美国网络星期一，成为全球最大的互联网的购物节日。

Xīfāng de gǎn'ēn jié shì yīgè wénhuà chuántǒng, tā qǐyuán yú běiměi tǔzhù xísú, tóngshí yěshì yīgè shìsú de jiérì. Zài gǎn'ēn jié, měiguó rén tōngcháng huì gòngxiǎng jiātíng jùcān hé guānkàn tèshū de tǐyù sàishì. Xiànzài tā yǐjīng yǎnbiàn chéngwéi yígè dà guīmó de shāngyè huódòng. Zài zhè yìtiān, xǔduō shāngdiàn hé shāngchǎng kāishǐ tóngshí zài xiànshàng xiànxià dǎzhé. Yìxiē shāngdiàn de dǎzhé huì yìzhí chíxù dào Wǎngluò Zhōu. Shíyī yuè zài Zhōngguó yěyǒu yígè dàxíng de huǒrè de dǎzhé cùxiāo huódòng. Táobǎo shāngchéng zài 2009 nián 11 yuè 11 rì tuīchūle yǐ "quán chǎng wǔ zhé, quánguó bāo yóu" zuòwéi cùxiāo kǒuhào de "táobǎo shāngchéng cùxiāo rì". Táobǎo shāngchéng jiāoyì é tūpò 5200 wàn yuán.2012 nián 11 yuè 11 rì wǎngluò gòuwù quánrì xiāoshòu é chāoguò Měiguó Wǎngluò Xīngqīyī, chéngwéi quánqiú zuìdà de hùliánwǎng de gòuwù jiérì.

Thanksgiving in the West is a cultural tradition that originated from the indigenous practices of North America, and is also a secular holiday. On Thanksgiving, Americans typically share family meals and watch special sporting events. Now it has evolved into a large-scale commercial event. On Black Friday, many stores and malls start online and offline sales at the same time. Discounts at some stores will continue through Cyber Week. There is also a large-scale hot discount promotion in China in November. On November 11, 2009, Taobao Mall launched the "Taobao Mall Promotion Day" with the promotion slogan "50% off the whole site, free shipping nationwide". The transaction volume of Taobao Mall exceeded 52 million yuan. On November 11, 2012, the full-day sales of online shopping surpassed Cyber Monday in the United States, becoming the world's busiest Internet shopping day.

生词/Vocabulary List

- 熟知 – shúzhī: familiar
- 感恩节 – gǎn'ēnjié: Thanksgiving
- 传统 – chuántǒng: tradition
- 起源 – qǐyuán: to originate
- 土著 – tǔzhù:indigenous
- 习俗 – xísú: custom, convention
- 长期 – chángqī: long-term
- 视为 – shì wéi: to be regarded as
- 世俗 – shìsú: secular, worldly
- 欧洲 – ōuzhōu: Europe
- 世纪 – shìjì: century
- 实践 – shíjiàn: to practice
- 早期 – zǎoqī: early period
- 形式 – xíngshì: form
- 感谢 – gǎnxiè: to thank, to appreciate
- 丰收 – fēngshōu: harvest
- 殖民者 – zhímín zhě: colonist
- 抵达 – dǐdá: to arrive
- 采用 – cǎiyòng: to use, to adopt
- 日期 – rìqī: date

- 庆祝 – qìngzhù: to celebrate
- 传统上 – chuántǒng shàng: traditionally
- 祝福 – zhùfú: to bless
- 丰收 – fēngshōu: harvest
- 通常 – tōngcháng: usually, typically
- 共享 – gòngxiǎng: shared
- 聚餐 – jùcān: to dine together
- 观看 – guānkàn: to watch
- 特殊 – tèshū: special
- 体育赛事 – tǐyù sàishì: sporting events
- 演变 – yǎnbiàn: to evolve
- 大规模 – dà guīmó: large-scale
- 著名 – zhùmíng: famous
- 标志 – biāozhì: to mark, to symbolize
- 商场 – shāngchǎng: shopping mall
- 线上 – xiànshàng: online
- 线下 – xiànxià: offline
- 打折 – dǎzhé: discount
- 网络 – wǎngluò: network
- 大型 – dàxíng: large-scale

- 火热 – huǒrè: literally meaning burning hot; popular in the context
- 促销 – cùxiāo: promotion
- 阿里巴巴 – Ālǐbābā: Alibaba
- 旗下 – qíxià: be a part of the umbrella company
- 淘宝 – táobǎo: Taobao
- 仿照 – fǎngzhào: to imitate
- 类似 – lèisì: similar
- 包邮 – bāoyóu: shipping included
- 口号 – kǒuhào: slogan
- 业界 – yèjiè: industry
- 淡季 – dànjì: off-season
- 交易额 – jiāoyì é: transaction amount
- 突破 – tūpò: to break through
- 日常 – rìcháng: daily
- 超过 – chāoguò: to exceed
- 互联网 – hùliánwǎng: the Internet

问题/Questions

1. 现在只有几个西方国家庆祝感恩节。

    Only a few Western countries now celebrate Thanksgiving.

    A. 对
    B. 错

2. 西方的感恩节起源于北美土著居民的习俗。

3. Thanksgiving in the West originated from the practices of the indigenous people
    in North America.

    A. 对
    B. 错

4. 在感恩节期间，以下哪项不适用？

    During the period of Thanksgiving, which of the following does not apply?

    A. 家人聚餐
    B. 参加街道游行
    C. 观看体育赛事

5. 淘宝商城在 2009 年 11 月 11 日推出了"全场五折，全国包邮"的促销日。

    On November 11, 2009, Taobao Mall launched a promotion day of "50% off on everything, free shipping nationwide".

    A. 对
    B. 错

6. 中国现在有全球最大的互联网购物日。

    China now has the world's busiest Internet shopping day.

    A. 对
    B. 错

答案/Answers

1. A 对
    True

2. A 对
    True

3. B 参加街道游行
    Attend street parade

4. A 对
    True

5. A 对
    True

CHAPTER 20

环境问题 – ENVIRONMENTAL ISSUES

很多人都喜欢**邀请**朋友来家里吃晚饭，**举办**一个**盛大**的**晚宴**。晚宴以前，主人会特别地**忙碌**。白天需要**打扫**房间，到各个大超市买吃的喝的，晚上还要**绞尽脑汁**地**考虑**准备哪些大菜。许多主人也会买鲜花、**葡萄酒**，甚至会提前**询问**客人对什么食物**过敏**。晚宴的时候，主人会**竭尽全力**地照顾好客人，**方方面面**都**料理**得很**周到**。

不过，晚宴后很多主人变得很**懒惰**。他们把**剩饭**和**垃圾**都**扔掉**。没有**精力**考虑哪些可以**回收**，哪些不可以。对自己的家主人**当然**很**重视**，有的主人还会请**钟点清洁工**来家里把**卫生彻彻底底**地打扫一遍，可是有几个主人会想他们应该怎样最好地**处理**晚宴**剩下**来的垃圾呢？

保护环境就**像**办一场晚宴。这个**程序**很长。我们生活的**地球**给我们**提供**了我们所需要的**一切**。现在地球上很多国家和**地区**的空气**污染**非常**严重**。我们在**街上**总是会看到很多垃圾。很多人**到处丢**垃圾，不关心他们的**行为**会不会影响环境。海洋里的鱼也是越来越少，**塑料袋反而**越来越多。

这个**情况**很**紧迫**，我们不能再这样**继续**生活下去了。**联合国**已经**介绍**了环境保护的**政策**。

根据环境保护专家，政府的**力度**还是**不够**。我们面对着一个**前所未有**的**挑战**，不可以再**依赖别人**来**解决**环境问题了。为了保护地球，我们每个人都应该尽一份我们自己的**责任**。

环境问题 – Environmental Issues
With English Translation

很多人都喜欢**邀请**朋友来家里吃晚饭，**举办**一个**盛大**的**晚宴**。

Hěnduō rén dōu xǐhuān **yāoqǐng** péngyǒu lái jiālǐ chī wǎnfàn, **jǔbàn** yígè **shèngdà** de **wǎnyàn**.

Many people like to **invite** friends over to their house for dinner and **host** a **grand dinner party**.

晚宴以前，主人会特别地**忙碌**。白天需要**打扫房间**，到各个大超市买吃的喝的，晚上还要**绞尽脑汁**地**考虑**准备哪些大菜。

Wǎnyàn yǐqián, zhǔrén huì tèbié de **mánglù**. Báitiān xūyào **dǎsǎo** fángjiān, dào gègè dà chāoshì mǎi chī de hē de, wǎnshang hái yào **jiǎojìnnǎozhī** de **kǎolǜ** zhǔnbèi nǎxiē dàcài.

Before the dinner, the hosts will be very **busy**. During the day, the hosts need to **clean** the room, go to various supermarkets to buy food and drink, and at night the hosts also need to **rack their brains** to **think** about the dishes to prepare.

许多主人也会买鲜花、**葡萄酒**，**甚至**会提前**询问**客人对什么食物**过敏**。晚宴的时候，主人会**竭尽全力**地照顾好客人，**方方面面**都**料理**得很周到。

Xǔduō zhǔrén yě huì mǎi xiānhuā, **pútáojiǔ**, **shènzhì** huì tíqián **xúnwèn** kèrén duì shénme shíwù **guòmǐn**. Wǎnyàn de shíhou, zhǔrén huì **jiéjìnquánlì** de zhàogù hǎo kèrén, **fāngfāngmiànmiàn** dōu **liàolǐ** dé hěn **zhōudào**.

Many hosts also buy flowers, **wine**, and **even ask** guests in advance what food **allergies** they have. During the dinner party, the hosts will **try their best** to take good care of the guests, and they are very **thoughtful in every aspect**.

不过，晚宴后很多主人变得很**懒惰**。他们把**剩饭**和**垃圾**都**扔掉**。没有**精力**考虑哪些可以**回收**，哪些不可以。

Búguò, wǎnyàn hòu hěnduō zhǔrén biàn dé hěn **lǎnduò**. Tāmen bǎ **shèng fàn** hé **lājī** dōu **rēng diào**. Méiyǒu **jīnglì** kǎolǜ nǎxiē kěyǐ **huíshōu**, nǎxiē bù kěyǐ.

After dinner, though, many hosts become **lazy**. They **throw away leftovers** and **rubbish**. They have no **energy** left to consider what can be **recycled** and what can't.

对自己的家主人**当然**很**重视**，有的主人还会请**钟点清洁工**来家里把**卫生彻彻底底**地打扫一遍，可是有几个主人会想他们应该怎样最好地**处理**晚宴**剩下来**的垃圾呢？

Duì zìjǐ de jiā zhǔrén **dāngrán** hěn **zhòngshì**, yǒu de zhǔrén hái huì qǐng **zhōngdiǎn qīngjié gōng** lái jiālǐ bǎ **wèishēng chèchè-dǐdǐ** de dǎsǎo yíbiàn, kěshì yǒu jǐ gè zhǔrén huì xiǎng tāmen yīnggāi zěnyàng zuì hǎo de **chǔlǐ** wǎnyàn **shèng xiàlái** de lājī ne?

The hosts **certainly pay great attention** to their own homes. Some hosts will also pay **hourly cleaners** to come and **clean** the house **thoroughly**, but how many hosts will think how they should best **handle** the garbage **left behind** from the dinner party?

保护环境就**像**办一场晚宴。这个**程序**很长。 我们生活的**地球**给我们**提供**了我们所需要的一切。

Bǎohù huánjìng jiù **xiàng** bàn yìchǎng wǎnyàn. Zhège **chéngxù** hěn cháng. Wǒmen shēnghuó de **dìqiú** gěi wǒmen **tígōng**le wǒmen suǒ xūyào de **yíqiè**.

Protecting the environment is **like** hosting a dinner party. This **process** is very long. The **earth** we live on **provides** us with everything we need.

228

现在地球上很多国家和**地区**的空气**污染**非常**严重**。我们在**街上**总是会看到很多垃圾。很多人**到处丢**垃圾，不关心他们的**行为**会不会影响环境。海洋里的**鱼**也是越来越少，**塑料袋反而**越来越多。

Xiànzài dìqiú shàng hěnduō guójiā hé **dìqū** de kōngqì **wūrǎn** fēicháng **yánzhòng**. Wǒmen zài **jiē shàng** zǒngshì huì kàn dào hěnduō lājī. Hěnduō rén **dàochù diū** lājī, bù guānxīn tāmen de **xíngwéi** huì bú huì yǐngxiǎng huánjìng. Hǎiyáng lǐ de yú yě shì yuè lái yuè shǎo, **sùliào dài** fǎn'ér yuè lái yuè duō.

Air **pollution** is very serious in many countries and regions on the planet. We always see a lot of garbage **on the street**. Many people **litter** and don't care if their **behavior** affects the environment. There are fewer and fewer fish in the ocean; **instead** there are more and more **plastic bags**.

这个**情况**很**紧迫**，我们不能再这样**继续**生活下去了。**联合国**已经介绍了环境保护的**政策**。

Zhège **qíngkuàng** hěn **jǐnpò**, wǒmen bùnéng zài zhèyàng **jìxù** shēnghuó xiàqùle. **Liánhéguó** yǐjīng **jièshào**le huánjìng bǎohù de **zhèngcè**.

This **situation** is **urgent**, and we cannot **continue** to live like this. **The United Nations** has already **introduced policies** for environmental protection.

在环境保护**专家**看来，政府的**力度**还是**不够**。我们**面对**着一个前**所未有**的**挑战**，不可以再**依赖别人**来**解决**环境问题了。

Zài huánjìng bǎohù zhuānjiā kàn lái, zhèngfǔ de lìdù háishì bùgòu. Wǒmen miànduì zhe yígè qiánsuǒwèiyǒu de tiǎozhàn, bù kěyǐ zài yīlài biérén lái jiějué huánjìng wèntí le.

According to environmental protection **experts**, the government's **efforts** are still **insufficient**. We **face** an **unprecedented challenge** and can no longer **rely on others** to **solve** environmental problems.

为了保护地球，我们每个人都应该尽一份我们自己的**责任**。

Wèile bǎohù dìqiú, wǒmen měi gè rén dōu yīnggāi **jìn** yífèn wǒmen zìjǐ de **zérèn**.

Each of us should **do** our part **in order to** protect the planet.

总结/Summary

保护环境就像办一场晚宴。这个程序很长。现在地球上很多国家和地区的空气污染非常严重。我们在街上总是会看到很多垃圾。很多人到处丢垃圾，不关心他们的行为会不会影响环境。海洋里的鱼也是越来越少，塑料袋反而越来越多。这个情况很紧迫，我们不能再这样继续生活下去了。我们面对着一个前所未有的挑战，不可以再依赖别人来解决环境问题了。为了保护地球，我们每个人都应该尽一份我们自己的责任。

Bǎohù huánjìng jiù xiàng bàn yìchǎng wǎnyàn. Zhège chéngxù hěn cháng. Xiànzài dìqiú shàng hěnduō guójiā hé dìqū de kōngqì wūrǎn fēicháng yánzhòng.Wǒmen zài jiē shàng zǒngshì huì kàn dào hěnduō lājī. Hěnduō rén dàochù diū lājī, bù guānxīn tāmen de xíngwéi huì bú huì yǐngxiǎng huánjìng.Hǎiyáng lǐ de yú yě shì yuè lái yuè shǎo, sùliào dài fǎn'ér yuè lái yuè duō. Zhège qíngkuàng hěn jǐnpò, wǒmen bùnéng zài zhèyàng jìxù shēnghuó xiàqùle. Wǒmen miànduìzhe yígè qiánsuǒwèiyǒu de tiǎozhàn, bù kěyǐ zài yīlài biérén lái jiějué huánjìng wèntí le. Wèile bǎohù dìqiú, wǒmen měi gè rén dōu yīnggāi jǐn yífèn wǒmen zìjǐ de zérèn.

Protecting the environment is like hosting a dinner party. This process is very long. Air pollution is very serious in many countries and regions on the earth. We always see a lot of garbage on the street. A lot of people litter and don't care if their actions affect the environment. There are fewer and fewer fish in the ocean, but more and more plastic bags. This situation is urgent, and we cannot continue to live like this. We face an unprecedented challenge and can no longer rely on others to solve environmental problems. Each of us should do our part to protect the planet.

生词/Vocabulary List

- 邀请 – yāoqǐng: to invite
- 举办 – jǔbàn: to hold
- 盛大 – shèngdà: grand
- 晚宴 – wǎnyàn: dinner
- 忙碌 – mánglù: busy
- 打扫 – dǎsǎo: to clean
- 绞尽脑汁 – jiǎojìnnǎozhī: to rack one's brains
- 考虑 – kǎolù: to consider, to think about
- 葡萄酒 – pútáojiǔ: wine
- 甚至 – shènzhì: even
- 询问 – xúnwèn: to ask
- 过敏 – guòmǐn: allergy
- 竭尽全力 – jiéjìnquánlì: make every effort
- 方方面面 – fāngfāngmiànmiàn: every aspect
- 料理 – liàolǐ: to manage
- 周到 – zhōudào: thoughtful, considerate
- 懒惰 – lǎnduò: lazy
- 剩饭 – shèng fàn: leftovers
- 垃圾 – lāji: rubbish
- 扔掉 – rēng diào: to throw away

- 精力 – jīnglì: energy
- 回收 – huíshōu: to recycle
- 当然 – dāngrán: certainly
- 钟点清洁工 – zhōngdiǎn qīngjié gōng: hourly cleaner
- 卫生 – wèishēng: health, sanitation
- 彻彻底底 – chèchè dǐdǐ: thoroughly
- 处理 – chǔlǐ: to deal with
- 剩下来 – shèng xiàlái: left over
- 保护 – bǎohù: to protect
- 环境 – huánjìng: environment, surroundings
- 像 – xiàng: be like
- 程序 – chéngxù: program
- 地球 – dìqiú: Earth
- 提供 – tígōng: to supply
- 一切 – yíqiè: everything
- 地区 – dìqū: area, region
- 污染 – wūrǎn: pollution
- 严重 – yánzhòng: serious, severe
- 街上 – jiē shàng: on the street
- 到处 – dàochù: everywhere

- 丢 – diū: to throw, to lose
- 行为 – xíngwéi: behavior
- 海洋 – hǎiyáng: ocean
- 塑料袋 – sùliào dài: plastic bag
- 反而 – fǎn'ér: instead
- 情况 – qíngkuàng: situation
- 紧迫 – jǐnpò: urgent
- 继续 – jìxù: to continue
- 联合国 – Liánhéguó: United Nations
- 介绍 – jièshào: to introduce
- 政策 – zhèngcè: policy
- 专家 – zhuānjiā: expert
- 力度 – lìdù: strength
- 不够 – búgòu: not enough
- 面对 – miàn duì: to face
- 前所未有 – qiánsuǒwèiyǒu: unprecedented
- 挑战 – tiǎozhàn: to challenge
- 依赖 – yīlài: to rely, to depend
- 别人 – biérén: other people
- 解决 – jiějué: to solve
- 为了 – wèile: in order to
- 责任 – zérèn: responsibility

问题/Questions

1. 很多国家和地区的空气污染非常严重。

   Air pollution in many countries and regions is very serious.

   A. 对
   B. 错

2. 晚宴后，主人总是会考虑哪些垃圾可以回收。

   After the dinner, the hosts always consider which garbage can be recycled.

   A. 对
   B. 错

3. 现在很多人到处丢垃圾。

   A lot of people litter nowadays.

   A. 对
   B. 错

4. 联合国还没有介绍环境保护的政策。

   The United Nations has not yet introduced policies on environmental protection.

   A. 对
   B. 错

5. 为了保护地球，我们每个人都应该尽一份我们自己的责任。

   Each of us should do our part to protect the planet.

   A. 对
   B. 错

答案/Answers

1. A 对
   True

2. B 错
   False

3. A 对
   True

4. B 错
   False

5. A 对
   True

CONCLUSION

We hope you've enjoyed reading our stories. Each chapter, as you will have noticed, was a story from daily life, a memorable event, or something educational.

Learning a language doesn't have to be a boring activity if you find suitable materials to learn with. Hopefully, we've provided you with some stories in Chinese that you find fun, engaging, and worthwhile to read. Feel free to use this book in the future when you need to revise vocabulary and expressions—we highly recommend it.

Believe in yourself and try to be a story writer yourself. Writing is a great way to consolidate every word and expression you have learned. It is also a creative process to encourage you to further expand your Chinese vocabulary.

P.S. Keep an eye out for more books like this one; we're not done teaching you Chinese! Head over to **www.LingoMastery.com** and read our articles and sign up for our newsletter. We give away so much free stuff that will accelerate your Chinese learning, and you don't want to miss that!

Printed in Great Britain
by Amazon

37911643R10139